C# & C++: The Beginner Guide

TABLE OF CONTENT

Before you start reading, scan this QR Code to get all bonus content!

PART 1: C++ BASICS

Welcome to Part 1: C++ Basics – the gateway to your exciting journey into the world of C++ programming! This section of the book has been carefully crafted to provide you with a comprehensive and easy-tounderstand introduction to the core concepts of C++. Whether you're a complete beginner stepping into the coding realm for the first time or an enthusiast looking to strengthen your programming prowess, this section will serve as a solid stepping stone.

In the chapters that follow, we'll walk you through the process of organizing up your C++ setup, ensuring you have the tools at your disposal to embark on this coding adventure with confidence. We'll demystify the various operations that C++ offers – from binary and arithmetic operations to relational comparisons – arming you with the skills needed to manipulate data effectively.

One of the highlights of C++ is its power in executing operations, making decisions, and controlling program flow. We'll delve into the world of C++ switches, loops, and decision-making structures, unraveling their functionality and showcasing how they can be harnessed to craft efficient and dynamic programs.

As you begin your journey, it's crucial to build a strong foundation. That's why we'll take the time to thoroughly explore the fundamental elements of C++. You'll become intimately familiar with the syntax, get comfortable with data types, and master the art of working with variables. By the time you reach the end of this section, you'll be equipped with the essential skills to tackle real-world coding challenges.

Furthermore, we understand that creating custom functions is a pivotal aspect of any programming language. In the later chapters of this section, you'll learn not only the how but also the why of creating your own functions in C++. We'll guide you through the process, ensuring you understand the ins and outs of function creation and how they enhance the modularity and reusability of your code.

So, whether you're excited to explore the historical significance of C++, curious about its evolution, or eager to write and run your very first C++ program, this section has something for you. We're thrilled to be your companions on this educational voyage. Let's begin this exciting chapter of your coding journey together!"

CHAPTER 1: INTRODUCTION TO C++ PROGRAMMING

Welcome to the world of C++ programming! In this chapter, we'll embark on a fascinating journey to explore the foundation and significance of C++ in the realm of software development. By the end of this chapter, you'll not only understand why C++ holds a special place in the programming landscape but also gain practical experience in setting up your development environment and running your first basic C++ program.

1.1 The Importance of C++ in Software Development

C++ stands as a cornerstone in the world of programming languages. Its impact on software development is profound, with a legacy that has shaped the modern coding landscape. From operating systems and game engines to high-performance applications, C++ has been a go-to choice for developers seeking efficiency, power, and control. The chapter will delve into the unique strengths of C++, shedding light on why it continues to be a preferred language for building robust and performant software.

1.2 History and Evolution of C++

To truly understand a programming language, it's essential to trace its origins and evolution. In this section, we'll journey through the history of C++, exploring its roots in the C programming language and how it evolved to become the feature-rich, versatile language it is today.

Understanding this evolution will provide you with insights into the design choices and motivations behind C++, setting the stage for your journey to master its concepts.

C++, an extension of the C programming language, was conceived in the late 1970s by Bjarne Stroustrup. Stroustrup, a Danish computer scientist, wanted to enhance the capabilities of the C language to better support object-oriented programming and systems programming.

1979: The roots of C++ can be traced back to 1979 when Bjarne

Stroustrup started working on "C with Classes." He aimed to introduce the concept of classes and objects to C, allowing for more structured and modular programming.

Early 1980s: As Stroustrup continued to refine his new language, it began to take shape as C++. The language retained the syntax and capabilities of C while incorporating the features of object-oriented programming, such as classes, objects, and inheritance.

1983: The first edition of the book "The C++ Programming Language" was published by Bjarne Stroustrup, serving as both a user manual and a documentation source for the language. This book played a crucial role in popularizing C++ and educating programmers about its concepts.

1985: The C++ language was standardized, leading to the release of the first official ANSI C++ standard in 1989. This marked an important milestone, as it provided a consistent framework for implementing C++ across different compilers and platforms.

1990s: Throughout the 1990s, C++ gained significant traction in various domains, including software development, systems programming, and game development. The language's versatility, efficiency, and support for both high-level and low-level programming made it a preferred choice for a wide range of applications.

2000s: C++ continued to evolve, with new features and enhancements introduced in subsequent standards. These standards, such as C++98, C++03, C++11, C++14, C++17, and C++20, brought improvements like standard libraries, lambda expressions, smart pointers, and more. The language continued to adapt to changing programming paradigms and the demands of modern software development.

Present and Beyond: As of September 2023, C++ remains a crucial programming language in various domains. Its ability to combine performance with high-level abstractions, along with ongoing standardization efforts, keeps C++ relevant and continuously evolving. The C++ community actively contributes to the language's growth, with discussions and proposals for further enhancements.

1.3 Set Up the Environment for Development

Before we dive into writing code, let's ensure you're set up for success. This section will guide you through the process of setting up your C++ development environment. From installing the necessary tools to configuring your system, we'll make sure you're ready to start coding without any hurdles. Whether you're using Windows, macOS, or a Linux distribution, we've got you covered.

Setting up a development environment for C++ involves several steps to ensure you have the necessary tools and configurations in place. Below is a general guide to help you get started:

1. Choose a Compiler:

The first step is to select a C++ compiler. Some popular choices include: - **GNU Compiler Collection (GCC):** Available on most platforms and widely used.

- **Microsoft Visual C++:** Windows-specific compiler, often used with Visual Studio IDE.
- **Clang:** A compiler that's known for its fast compilation times and helpful error messages.

2. Install the Compiler:

Depending on your choice of compiler, follow the installation instructions for your operating system:

- For GCC: On Linux, GCC is usually pre-installed. On Windows, you can use MinGW or MSYS2 to install GCC.

- For Visual C++: Install Visual Studio, a powerful IDE that includes the compiler and various development tools.
- For Clang: Instructions can vary based on the platform, but prebuilt binaries are often available.

3. Integrated Development Environment (IDE) Setup: While not strictly necessary, using an IDE can greatly simplify development. Here's how to set up a basic environment using Visual Studio Code as an example:

- **Install Visual Studio Code:** Download and install Visual Studio Code from its official website.
- **Install Extensions:** Install the C/C++ which is called an extension by Microsoft from the Visual Studio Code Extensions marketplace. This extension provides features like code highlighting, autocompletion, and debugging.

Remember that these instructions are generalized and can vary based on your operating system and specific tools. Always check the official documentation for your compiler and IDE you choose for accurate installation and setup instructions.

1.4 Writing and Running a Basic C++ Program

The best way to kick off your C++ journey is by writing your first program. In this section, you'll learn the fundamental structure of a C++ program. We'll guide you through the process of writing a simple "Hello, World!" program, explaining each component along the way. You'll discover how to compile and run your program, gaining hands-on experience in executing C++ code.

By the end of this chapter, you'll have a solid grasp of why C++ holds such significance in the software development landscape. You'll also be equipped with the tools and knowledge to write and run basic C++ programs, setting the stage for your exploration of this versatile and powerful programming language.

1. Open a Text Editor or Integrated Development Environment (IDE):

Start by launching a text editor or an Integrated Development Environment

(IDE) where you can write your C++ code. Common choices include Visual Studio Code, Sublime Text, Code::Blocks, Dev-C++, and many others.

2. Create a New C++ Source File:

In your chosen editor or IDE, create a new source code file with a `.cpp` extension. This extension indicates that the file contains C++ source code. For example, you could create a file named `hello.cpp`.

3. Write Your C++ Code:

Inside the `.cpp` file, write your C++ code. Here's a simple "Hello, World!" program as an example:

```cpp
#include <iostream>

int main() {
    std::cout << "Hello, World!" << std::endl;
    return 0;
}
```

In this program, `#include <iostream>` includes the necessary header to use input/output stream operations. The `main()` function is the entry point of the program, and it outputs "Hello, World!" to the console using

`std::cout`.

4. Save the File:

Save the `.cpp` file after writing the code. Ensure that the file name and extension match, like `hello.cpp`.

5. Open a Terminal or Command Prompt:

To compile and run the program, you need to use a terminal or command prompt. On Windows, you can use Command Prompt or PowerShell. On macOS and Linux, you can use the terminal.

6. Navigate to the File Location:

Navigate to the `cd` command to find the directory where you saved the `.cpp` file. For example, if the file is on your desktop, you might use:

```
cd Desktop
```

---

7. Compile the Program:

Compile the C++ program using a compiler. The command and compiler you use depend on your platform and preferences.

- If you're using `g++`, the GNU C++ compiler, you can compile the program with:

```
g++ -o hello hello.cpp
```

This command compiles `hello.cpp` and creates an executable named `hello`.

8. Run the Compiled Program:

After compiling, you can run the compiled program. For example:

- On Windows, if you compiled with g++, you would run:

```
hello.exe
```

- On macOS or Linux, you would run:

```
./hello
```

9. See the Output:

Once you boot up the program, you'll see the output in the terminal. In this case, you'll see:

```
Hello, World!
```

Congratulations! You've successfully written, compiled, and executed your first C++ program.

Remember that specific commands may vary depending on your operating system and the compiler you're using. Always consult the documentation for the compiler you've chosen for accurate information.

1.5 The Significance Of Installation & Running Your First Program

The initial installation of C++ and the significance of running your first program, even if it's basic, are foundational steps that serve crucial purposes in the world of programming education and development. Let's explore the importance of these aspects:

1. Initial Installation of C++:

- **Access to Tools:** Installing a C++ compiler provides you with the essential tools needed to write, compile, and run C++ code. These tools include the compiler itself, libraries, and utilities that help you transform your code into executable programs.
- **Creating a Development Environment:** A properly installed C++ environment sets up the foundation for your programming journey. It ensures you have a suitable workspace where you can experiment, learn, and build projects.
- **Consistency:** By using established compilers and development environments, you ensure that your code will work consistently across different systems. This is especially important when collaborating with others or sharing your work.

2. Significance of Running Your First Program:

- **Building Confidence:** Running your first program, no matter how basic, can be an incredibly empowering experience. It gives you a sense of accomplishment and boosts your confidence in your ability to understand and manipulate the programming environment.
- **Understanding the Workflow:** The process of writing, compiling, and running code introduces you to the typical development workflow. This workflow is fundamental to programming, and mastering it early on sets you up for success in more complex projects.
- **Debugging and Problem-Solving:** Even a simple program can have errors or unexpected behavior. Learning to run and analyze your code allows you to identify issues, understand error messages, and start building the problem-solving skills necessary in programming.
- **Practicing Basics:** Basic programs often involve fundamental concepts like syntax, variables, and output. Running these programs helps you solidify your understanding of these building blocks, which you'll continue to use in more advanced coding tasks.
- **Transitioning to Complexity:** Running a simple program is the first step toward working with larger, more intricate projects. As you progress, you'll be better equipped to handle the challenges of more complex code.

In essence, the initial installation and running of your first program mark the beginning of your programming journey. They lay the groundwork for your understanding of the development environment, coding concepts, and the process of turning your ideas into executable software. Whether you're a beginner or a seasoned programmer, these steps remain essential and are part of every coder's story. Now, it's time to get into the nitty gritty! In Chapter 2, we dive deeper into the world of C++, so buckle up, and get ready to learn!

CHAPTER 2: C++ FUNDAMENTALS

Welcome to Chapter 2: C++ Fundamentals! In this chapter, we will dive deeper into the core concepts of C++ programming. By the end of this chapter, you'll have a solid grasp of variables, data types, operators, control structures, functions, parameters, return values, and the scope of variables.

2.1 Variables, Data Types, and Operators

Variables: We'll start by introducing the concept of variables – placeholders for storing and manipulating data. You'll learn how to declare variables, assign values, and understand their role in programming.

Introduction to Variables in C++

Variables are essential components in programming that allow you to store and manipulate data. They act as named storage locations in your computer's memory, enabling you to work with information such as numbers, text, and more. Think of variables as containers that hold values you can use and modify within your program.

Declaring Variables:

In C++, declaring a variable involves specifying its type and giving it a name. The type defines the kind of data the variable will hold, such as an integer, a floating-point number, or a character.

Here's how you declare a variable:

```
// Syntax: data_type variable_name;
int age;            // Declare an integer variable named "age"
double price;       // Declare a floating-point variable named "price"
char grade;         // Declare a character variable named "grade"
```

Assigning Values to Variables:

After declaring a variable, you can assign a value to it using the assignment operator (`=`). The value should match the variable's data type.

Here's how you assign values to variables:

```
age = 25;          // Assign the value 25 to the "age" variable
price = 19.99;     // Assign the value 19.99 to the "price" variable
grade = 'A';       // Assign the character 'A' to the "grade" variable
```

You can also combine declaration and assignment in a single step:

```
int quantity = 10;          // Declare and assign the value 10 to "quantity"
double temperature = 75.5; // Declare and assign the value 75.5 to "temperature"
char symbol = '$';          // Declare and assign the character '$' to "symbol"
```

Understanding the Role of Variables:

Variables play a vital role in programming by allowing you to:

- **Store Data:** Variables store information that your program needs to work with. This could be user input, calculated values, or constants. - **Manipulate Data:** You can perform calculations, modifications, and transformations on the data stored in variables. For example, adding numbers, concatenating strings, or comparing values.
- **Enable Flexibility:** Variables enable your program to adapt and respond dynamically to changing conditions and user interactions.
- **Enhance Readability:** Giving meaningful names to variables improves code readability and makes your intentions clear.
- **Reuse Values:** Once you've stored a value in a variable, you can use it multiple times throughout your program without having to re-enter or recalculate it.

In summary, variables are the foundation of any program, enabling you to work with data in a flexible and organized manner. By declaring, assigning, and utilizing variables effectively, you can create powerful and dynamic programs tailored to specific tasks and requirements.

Data Types: C++ supports various data types, each with its own purpose and storage requirements. We'll explore fundamental types like integers, floating-point numbers, characters, and more.

In C++, data types are utilized to specify which types of data that a variable may hold. Each data type has its own set of values, storage requirements, and operations that can be performed on it. Here are some fundamental data types in C++:

1. Integers:

Integers represent whole numbers without decimal points. C++ provides various sizes of integer data types:

- *int*: Represents signed integers, typically using 4 bytes.
- *short int*: Represents smaller signed integers, often using 2 bytes.
- *long int*: Represents larger signed integers, commonly using 4 or 8 bytes.
- *long long int*: Represents very large signed integers, introduced in C++11.

2. Floating-Point Numbers:

Floating-point numbers are used to represent decimal values. C++ offers two primary floating-point data types:

- *float*: Represents single-precision floating-point numbers, typically using 4 bytes.
- *double*: Represents double-precision floating-point numbers, often using 8 bytes.

3. Characters:

Characters represent individual characters, such as letters, digits, or symbols. C++ provides the `char` data type to store characters. For example:

```
char letter = 'A'; // Single character enclosed in single quotes
```

4. Boolean:

Let's be clear that `bool` data type will represent boolean values, which can be either `true` or `false`. Boolean values are crucial for making decisions in conditional statements. For example:

```
bool isTrue  = true;
bool isFalse = false;
```

5. Strings:

Strings are sequences of characters. In C++, strings are not a built-in data type, but you can use the Standard Template Library (STL) `std::string` class to work with strings. For example:

```
#include <string>
std::string name = "Alice";
```

6. Other Data Types:

C++ offers more data types, such as `unsigned int` (for non-negative integers), `wchar_t` (for wide characters), and custom user-defined types through classes and structures.

7. Size and Portability:

The storage requirements for each data type can vary based on the system and compiler. The C++ standard provides guidelines on the minimum size of each data type, ensuring portability across different platforms.

8. Type Modifiers:

You can modify the size or behavior of data types using type modifiers like `unsigned`, `signed`, `long`, and `short`. For instance, `unsigned int` represents non-negative integers.

Understanding data types is crucial because they determine the range of values a variable can hold and the operations that can be performed on those values. By choosing the appropriate data type for your variables, you optimize memory usage and ensure accurate calculations in your programs.

Operators: Operators are essential for performing operations on variables and values. We'll cover arithmetic, assignment, comparison, logical, and bitwise operators, showing how they help manipulate data effectively.

Operators in C++

Operators are symbols that represent actions or computations on variables and values. They allow you to perform a wide range of operations, from basic arithmetic calculations to complex logical evaluations. Operators are essential because they facilitate data manipulation and enable you to create dynamic and interactive programs.

Arithmetic Operators:

Arithmetic operators will run basic mathematical operations on all numeric data types:

- `+`: Addition
- `-`: Subtraction
- `*`: Multiplication
- `/`: Division
- `%`: Modulus (remainder after division)

Assignment Operators:

Assignment operators are used to assign values to variables:

- `=`: Assigns the value on the right to the variable on the left.
- `+=`, `-=`, `*=`, `/=`, `%=`: Combine an operation with assignment. For example, `x += 5` is equivalent to `x = x + 5`.

Comparison Operators:

Comparison operators are used to compare two values and evaluate expressions:

- `==`: Equal to
- `!=`: Not equal to
- `<`: Less than
- `>`: Greater than
- `<=`: Less than or equal to
- `>=`: Greater than or equal to

Logical Operators:

Logical operators are utilized to make and combine multiple conditions and then evaluate the results:

- `&&`: Logical AND (returns `true` if both conditions are `true`) - `||`: Logical OR (returns `true` if at least one condition is `true`) - `!`: Logical NOT (negates the result of a condition)

Bitwise Operators:

Bitwise operators perform operations on individual bits of integer values:

- `&`: Bitwise AND
- `|`: Bitwise OR
- `^`: Bitwise XOR (exclusive OR)
- `~`: Bitwise NOT (flips the bits)
- `<<`: Left shift (shifts bits to the left) - `>>`: Right shift (shifts bits to the right)

Importance of Operators:

Operators are crucial because they enable you to:

- Perform calculations: Arithmetic operators let you manipulate numeric values to perform calculations and mathematical operations. - Make decisions: Comparison and logical operators are essential for creating conditional statements that make decisions based on conditions. - Assign values: Assignment operators help you store and update values in variables.
- Manipulate bits: Bitwise operators are useful for low-level operations, such as working with binary representations of data.

By using operators effectively, you can build complex expressions, control program flow, and create dynamic behaviors in your code. They are the building blocks that empower you to work with data and create programs that interact with users, perform computations, and achieve various tasks.

CHAPTER 3: CONTROL STRUCTURES

Control Structures: if Statements, Loops, Switches

if Statements: Conditional statements allow your program to make decisions based on conditions. We'll explain the syntax of the `if` statement and show how it controls the flow of your program.

The `if` statement is a fundamental control structure in C++ that allows you to make decisions in your program based on a condition. It controls the flow of your program by executing a certain block of code only if the specified condition is true.

Syntax of the `if` Statement:

The basic syntax of the `if` statement is as follows:

```
if (condition) {
    // Code to execute if the condition is true
}
```

Here's how it works:

1. The keyword `if` indicates the start of the conditional statement.
2. The condition is enclosed in parentheses (`()`). It's an expression that evaluates to either `true` or `false`.
3. If the condition is true, the code block inside the curly braces `{}` is executed. If the condition is false, the code block is skipped.

Example: Using the `if` Statement:

Let's see a practical example. Suppose we want to determine whether a given number is positive. If it is, we'll display a message indicating that it's positive.

```
#include <iostream>

int main() {
    int number;

    std::cout << "Enter a number: ";
    std::cin >> number;

    if (number > 0) {
        std::cout << "The number is positive." << std::endl;
    }

    return 0;
}
```

In this example:

- We declare an integer variable `number` to store the user's input.
- We prompt the user to enter a number using `std::cin`.
- The `if` statement checks whether the `number` is greater than 0. - If the condition is true, the message "The number is positive." is displayed.

Flow Control:

The `if` statement controls the flow of your program by allowing certain code blocks to be executed conditionally. If the condition specified in the `if` statement evaluates to true, the code within the associated block of curly braces is executed. If false, it is skipped entirely.

This flow control enables you to create dynamic behavior in your program. You can have multiple `if` statements, combine them with `else` and `else if` clauses, and create intricate decision-making processes.

In summary, the `if` statement is a powerful tool for controlling program flow based on conditions. It empowers you to create logic that adapts to different situations, making your programs more interactive and responsive.

Loops: Loops are crucial for executing a block of code repeatedly. We'll discuss `while`, `do-while`, and `for` loops, demonstrating how to use them to automate repetitive tasks.

Loops are crucial in programming because they allow you to execute a block of code repeatedly, automating repetitive tasks and saving you from writing redundant code. Different types of loops offer varying levels of control over the repetition process. Let's discuss *`while`*, *`do-while`*, and *`for`* loops and how to use them effectively:

1. `while` Loop:

Syntax:

```
while (condition) {
    // Code to repeat
}
```

Example: Using a `while` Loop:

```
#include <iostream>

int main() {
    int count = 0;
    while (count < 5) {
        std::cout << "Count: " << count << std::endl;
        count++;
    }
    return 0;
}
```

2. `do-while` Loop:

The `do-while` loop is just like the `while` loop, but it guarantees that the block of code is executed at least once, regardless of whether the condition is initially true or false.

Syntax:

```
do {
    // Code to repeat
} while (condition);
```

Example: Using a `do-while` Loop:

```
#include <iostream>

int main() {
    int count = 0;

    do {
        std::cout << "Count: " << count << std::endl;
        count++;
    } while (count < 5);

    return 0;
}
```

3. `for`Loop:

The `for` loop is designed for iterating a specific number of times. It consists of an initialization step, a condition, and an update statement.

Syntax:

```
for (initialization; condition; update) {
    // Code to repeat
}
```

Example: Using a `for` Loop:

```
#include <iostream>

int main() {
    for (int i = 0; i < 5; i++) {
        std::cout << "Count: " << i << std::endl;
    }

    return 0;
}
```

Importance of Loops:

- **Efficiency**: Loops save you from manually repeating the same code over and over. They allow you to execute a block of code as many times as needed without duplicating code.
- **Automation**: Loops are essential for automating repetitive tasks, such as processing lists of data or iterating over collections.
- **Dynamic Behavior**: Loops enable your program to adapt to different situations and handle varying amounts of data or input. - **Structured Code**: Loops promote clean and organized code by encapsulating repetitive logic within a single block.

When choosing a loop type, consider the nature of the task and the condition under which you want the loop to execute. `*while*` and `*do-while*` loops are suitable when the number of iterations is unknown, while `*for*` loops are ideal for a known number of iterations.

In summary, loops are a fundamental part of programming that enable you to efficiently handle repetitive tasks and make your code more dynamic and adaptable.

Switch Statements: Switch statements provide an elegant way to handle multiple conditions. We'll guide you through the usage of `switch` and `case` to streamline decision-making.

Switch statements provide an elegant way to handle multiple conditions in a structured and efficient manner. They are particularly useful when you have a single variable or expression whose value you want to compare against several possible constant values. Switch statements improve code readability and help streamline decision-making.

Advantages of Switch Statements:

1. **Readability**: Switch statements make the code more readable by clearly indicating that you're evaluating different cases for a single variable.
2. **Efficiency**: Switch statements are often more efficient than using a series of `if` statements when comparing a variable against multiple constant values.
3. **Logical Flow**: Switch statements enforce a logical flow by preventing execution of unnecessary code blocks after a match is found.

Usage of `switch` and `case`:

Syntax of a Switch Statement:

```
switch (expression) {
    case value1:
        // Code to execute if expression == value1
        break;
    case value2:
        // Code to execute if expression == value2
        break;
    // ...
    default:
        // Code to execute if no case matches
}
```

- The `switch` keyword starts the statement, followed by the expression you want to evaluate.
- Each `case` label specifies a constant value to compare against the expression.
- The `break` statement terminates the switch statement and prevents execution of subsequent cases.
- The `default` case is optional and executes when none of the `case` values match the expression.

Example of Using a `switch` Statement:

```cpp
#include <iostream>

int main() {
    int day = 3;

    switch (day) {
        case 1:
            std::cout << "Monday" <<
std::endl;
            break;
        case 2:
            std::cout << "Tuesday" <<
std::endl;
            break;
        case 3:
            std::cout << "Wednesday"
<< std::endl;
            break;
        case 4:
            std::cout << "Thursday" <<
std::endl;
            break;
        case 5:
            std::cout << "Friday" <<
std::endl;
            break;
        default:
            std::cout << "Invalid day"
<< std::endl;
    }

    return 0;
}
```

In this example:

- The `switch` statement evaluates the value of the `day` variable. - If `day` equals 3, the code within the `case 3:` block is executed (`"Wednesday"` is printed).
- The `break` statement ends the `switch` block.
- If `day` doesn't match any of the `case` values, the `default` case is executed (`"Invalid day"` is printed).

Switch statements are especially useful when you have a discrete set of possible values to compare, making your code more concise and easier to maintain.

2.3 Functions, Parameters, and Return Values

Functions: Functions allow you to modularize your code into manageable blocks. You'll learn how to declare, define, and call functions, improving code organization and reusability.

Functions are a fundamental concept in programming that allow you to modularize your code into manageable blocks. They offer a way to break down your program's logic into smaller, self-contained units that can be easily understood, organized, and reused. Let's explore how functions work, including their declaration, definition, and usage, to improve code organization and reusability.

Modularizing with Functions:

Functions enable you to divide your program's functionality into smaller, logical units. Each function performs a specific task or operation, and you can group related functions together. This modular approach enhances code readability, maintainability, and reusability.

Declaration and Definition of Functions:

Declaration:

A function declaration gives the compiler with all of the information about the function's name, return type, and parameter list. It tells the compiler what the function looks like without providing the actual implementation.

Syntax of Declaration:

```
return_type function_name(parameter_type parameter_name, ...);
```

Definition:

A function definition will always contain the actual implementation of the function. It includes the code that will be executed when the function is called.

Syntax of Definition:

```
return_type function_name(parameter_type parameter_name, ...) {
    // Function implementation
    // ...
}
```

Example of Declaring and Defining a Function:

```
#include <iostream>

// Function Declaration
int add(int a, int b);

int main() {
    int result = add(3, 5);
    std::cout << "Result: " << result << std::endl;
    return 0;
}

// Function Definition
int add(int a, int b) {
    return a + b;
}
```

Function Calls:

To use a function, you call it by its name and provide the necessary arguments. The function then executes its code and may return a value.

Syntax of Function Call:

```
return_type result = function_name(argument1, argument2, ...);
```

Example of Calling a Function:

```
#include <iostream>

int multiply(int x, int y) {
    return x * y;
}

int main() {
    int product = multiply(4, 6);
    std::cout << "Product: " << product << std::endl
    return 0;
}
```

Benefits of Using Functions:

1. **Code Reusability**: it's cool that if a function would be defined, you can call it multiple times from different parts of your program, reducing redundancy.
2. **Modularity:** Functions allow you to encapsulate specific tasks, making your code more organized and easier to manage.
3. **Readability:** Well-named functions make your code more readable by giving meaningful context to each operation.
4. **Maintenance:** If a change is needed, you can update the function's implementation without affecting other parts of the code.
5. **Collaboration**: Functions enable multiple developers to work on different parts of a program simultaneously.

In essence, functions provide a way to structure your code into smaller, self-contained units, making your programs more organized, maintainable, and reusable.

Parameters: Functions can accept input parameters, which enhance their flexibility. We'll explore how to pass arguments to functions, enabling dynamic behavior.

Parameters in functions are placeholders that allow you to pass values to the function when it's called. They enable dynamic behavior by allowing you to provide different data to the same function, making it more versatile and adaptable. Let's explore how parameters work and how to pass arguments to functions.

Parameters in Functions:

Parameters are variables that you define within the parentheses of a function's declaration. They act as placeholders for the values that you'll pass to the function when you call it. These values are known as arguments.

Syntax of Function Declaration with Parameters:

```
return_type function_name(parameter_type parameter_name, ...);
```

Example of a Function with Parameters:

```
#include <iostream>
void greet(std::string name) {
    std::cout << "Hello, " << name << "!" << std::endl;
}

int main() {
    greet("Alice");
    greet("Bob");
    return 0;
}
```

In this example, the function `greet` takes a parameter named `name`, which represents the name of the person being greeted. If the function is called, we see that the argument `"Alice"` is then passed to the `name` parameter the first time, and `"Bob"` the second time.

Passing Arguments to Functions:

When you call a function that has parameters, you provide values (arguments) that match the types of the parameters. These arguments are passed to the function and can be used within its code block.

Syntax of Function Call with Arguments:

```
function_name(argument1, argument2, ...);
```

Example of Passing Arguments to a Function:

```
#include <iostream>

void printSum(int a, int b) {
    int sum = a + b;
    std::cout << "Sum: " << sum << std::endl;
}

int main() {
    printSum(3, 7); // Calling the function with arguments 3 and 7
    return 0;
}
```

We see that the `printSum` function can take two integer parameters, `a` and `b`. When the function is called with `printSum(3, 7)`, the values `3` and `7` are passed as arguments. Inside the function, these values are assigned to `a` and `b`, and their sum is printed.

Benefits of Using Parameters:

1. **Dynamic Behavior**: Parameters enable you to create dynamic and adaptable functions that can work with different input data, enhancing the versatility of your code.
2. **Reusability**: By using parameters, you can create a single function that performs a specific operation on different data, reducing code duplication. **3. Customization:** Functions with parameters allow you to customize the behavior of the function based on the values you provide.

4. Abstraction: Parameters abstract the input data from the function's internal implementation, making the function more focused and clear.

In summary, parameters in functions enable you to create flexible, reusable, and dynamic code by allowing you to pass values (arguments) to functions when they are called. This customization is essential for creating functions that can handle various scenarios and inputs.

Return Values: Functions can also produce output through return values. We'll demonstrate how to return values from functions and utilize them in your programs.

Functions can not only receive input through parameters but also produce output through return values. A return value is the data that a function sends back to the caller after it completes its execution. This allows functions to perform calculations or operations and provide their results to the rest of the program. Let's explore how to return values from functions and utilize them in your programs.

Syntax of Function Declaration with Return Type:

```
return_type function_name(parameter_type parameter_name, ...)
```

Syntax of Returning a Value from a Function:

```
return_type function_name(parameter_type parameter_name, ...
    // Function implementation
    // ...
    return value_to_return;
}
```

Example of Returning a Value from a Function:

```
#include <iostream>

int add(int a, int b) {
    int sum = a + b;
    return sum;
}

int main() {
    int result = add(3, 5);
    std::cout << "Sum: " << result << std::endl;
    return 0;
}
```

Utilizing Return Values:

Return values can be used in various ways within your program. They can be assigned to variables, used in expressions, or even passed as arguments to other functions.

Example of Using a Return Value in an Expression:

```
#include <iostream>

int multiply(int x, int y) {
    return x * y;
}

int main() {
    int product = multiply(4, 6);
    int tripleProduct = 3 * product; // Using the returned value in an expression
    std::cout << "Triple of the product: " << tripleProduct << std::endl;
    return 0;
}
```

In this example, the returned value from the `multiply` function is assigned to the `product` variable. The value is then used to calculate the triple of the product.

Benefits of Return Values:

1. Data Sharing: Return values allow functions to communicate results back to the caller, enabling the reuse of calculated or processed data. **2. Modularization**: Functions with return values can be thought of as "black boxes" that perform a specific task and provide a result, promoting modular code design.

3. Complex Operations: Functions with return values can encapsulate complex calculations or operations, making your main program logic cleaner and easier to understand.

In summary, functions that return values provide a way to encapsulate operations and calculations within functions while allowing them to interact with the rest of the program. This enhances code organization and reusability by enabling you to create functions that produce specific results that can be used throughout your code.

CHAPTER 4: SCOPE AND LOCAL/GLOBAL VARIABLES

Variable Scope: Variables have scope – the region of code where they are accessible. We'll explain the concepts of local and global scope, highlighting their impact on variable visibility.

The concept of variable scope refers to the region of code where a variable can be accessed or manipulated. Depending on where a variable is declared, it can have different levels of visibility and lifetime within your program. There are two main types of scope: local scope and global scope.

Local Scope:

A variable declared within a block of code, such as within a function or a loop, has local scope. It's accessible only within that specific block where it's defined. Once the block is exited, the variable goes out of scope and cannot be accessed anymore.

Example of Local Scope:

```
#include <iostream>
int main() {
    int x = 5; // x has local scope within the main function
    std::cout << x << std::endl; // x is accessible here
    {
        int y = 10; // y has local scope within this block
        std::cout << y << std::endl; // y is accessible here
    }
    // Cannot access y here (out of scope)
    return 0;
}
```

In this example, `x` is declared within the `main` function, making it accessible throughout the function. `y`, on the other hand, is declared within a nested block and is only accessible within that block.

Global Scope:

A variable declared outside of any block of code (usually at the beginning of the program) has global scope. It's visible and accessible from any part of the program, including all functions, loops, and blocks.

Example of Global Scope:

```
#include <iostream>

int globalVariable = 100; // globalVariable has global scope

void printGlobal() {
    std::cout << globalVariable << std::endl; // globalVariable is accessible
here
}

int main() {
    std::cout << globalVariable << std::endl; // globalVariable is accessible
here
    printGlobal();
    return 0;
}
```

In this example, `globalVariable` is declared at the top of the program, giving it global scope. It can be accessed both within the `main` function and within the `printGlobal` function.

Impact on Variable Visibility:

- **Local Scope:** Variables with local scope are useful when you want to encapsulate data within a specific context. They prevent unintended interactions between different parts of your program by limiting the visibility of the variable to its block of declaration. This helps maintain data integrity and minimizes unintended side effects.
- **Global Scope:** Variables with global scope are accessible from anywhere in your program, which can be convenient for sharing data across functions or modules. However, they can also make your code less modular and harder to maintain, as changes to a global variable's value can affect multiple parts of your program.

Choosing the appropriate scope for your variables depends on the intended use and the desired level of encapsulation. It's generally recommended to limit the scope of variables whenever possible to improve code organization and prevent unintended side effects.

Local Variables: Local variables are declared within a specific scope. We'll discuss their advantages, including encapsulation and avoiding naming conflicts.

Local variables are variables that are declared within a specific scope, such as within a function, loop, or block of code. They have limited visibility and are only accessible within the scope in which they are defined. Local variables offer several advantages, including encapsulation and avoiding naming conflicts.

Declaring Local Variables:

Local variables are declared by specifying the variable's data type and name within the scope where they will be used. Once declared, they can be assigned values and manipulated within that scope.

Example of Declaring and Using Local Variables:

```
#include <iostream>

void printNumber() {
    int num = 42; // num is a local variable within the function
    std::cout << "Number: " << num << std::endl;
}

int main() {
    int x = 10; // x is a local variable within the main function
    printNumber();
    return 0;
}
```

In this example, `num` is a local variable declared within the `printNumber` function. It's accessible only within that function. Similarly, `x` is a local variable declared within the `main` function. Each variable is confined to its respective scope.

Advantages of Local Variables:

1. **Encapsulation**: Local variables promote encapsulation by limiting the visibility of variables to specific blocks of code. This ensures that variables are used only in the context for which they are intended.
2. **Reduced Naming Conflicts**: Since local variables are confined to their respective scopes, you can reuse variable names in different parts of your program without causing naming conflicts. This enhances code organization and makes your codebase more manageable.
3. **Data Integrity**: Local variables prevent unintended interference from other parts of your program. Changes made to a local variable within one scope won't affect the same-named local variables in other scopes.
4. **Clearer Code**: Using local variables within smaller, specific scopes enhances code clarity and readability. Readers can quickly understand where a variable is used and what it represents.

Encapsulation and Avoiding Naming Conflicts:

Local variables shine in scenarios where you want to encapsulate data within a specific function or block. This encapsulation ensures that the variable's value is only relevant and visible within its intended context, preventing accidental misuse or changes from other parts of the program.

Furthermore, local variables help you avoid naming conflicts. You can use the same variable names in different functions or blocks without worrying about unintended interactions. Each local variable's name is unique within its scope, allowing you to keep your codebase organized and easy to understand.

In summary, local variables provide encapsulation and prevent naming conflicts, making your code more modular, maintainable, and organized. They ensure that data is used within the intended scope and help avoid unintended side effects caused by the use of common variable names.

Global Variables: Global variables have broader visibility but come with certain considerations. We'll explore their usage and potential drawbacks.

Global variables are variables that are defined at the top level of a program, outside of any specific function or block. They have a global scope, which means they can be accessed from any part of the program, including different functions, loops, and blocks. While global variables can be useful in certain situations, they also come with potential drawbacks.

Usage of Global Variables:

1. **Sharing Data**: Global variables can be used to share data among multiple functions or modules within a program. This can simplify data exchange and reduce the need to pass data through function parameters.
2. **Configuration Settings**: Global variables can store configuration settings or constants that need to be accessed and used across various parts of the program.
3. **Constants:** Global variables can hold constants that remain consistent throughout the program's execution, providing a central place to manage and update them.

Potential Drawbacks of Global Variables:

1. **Reduced Modularity**: Excessive use of global variables can lead to decreased modularity, making it harder to understand the relationships between different parts of the program. Functions that depend on global variables become tightly coupled and less reusable.
2. **Unintended Side Effects:** Modifications to global variables can have unintended side effects on other parts of the program. This can lead to unexpected behavior that is difficult to diagnose and fix.
3. **Naming Conflicts:** If multiple parts of the program use the same global variable names, conflicts can arise, causing confusion and errors.
4. **Debugging Complexity**: Debugging becomes more challenging when global variables are involved. Identifying the source of changes to global variables can be difficult in larger codebases.
5. **Thread Safety:** In multi-threaded programs, global variables can lead to synchronization problems if not handled carefully. Concurrent access to global variables can result in data races and unpredictable behavior.

Best Practices:

If you decide to use global variables, here are some best practices to consider:

1. **Limit Their Use:** Use global variables sparingly and only when necessary. Minimize their impact on the overall codebase.

2. **Make Them Constants**: If possible, define global variables as constants to ensure they are not accidentally modified.

3. **Use Descriptive Names:** Give meaningful names to global variables to make their purpose clear and minimize the risk of naming conflicts.

4. **Document Their Purpose**: Provide comments or documentation that explains the purpose and usage of each global variable.

5. **Encapsulation**: Whenever possible, encapsulate related data and functionality in classes or modules, reducing the need for global variables.

6. **Consider Alternatives:** Explore alternatives such as passing parameters or using function return values to share data between functions.

Global variables can provide convenience by allowing data to be accessed from various parts of a program. However, they should be used with caution due to their potential drawbacks, including reduced modularity, unintended side effects, and naming conflicts. As a best practice, consider using alternative approaches to data sharing and design your program in a way that minimizes reliance on global variables.

CHAPTER 5: OBJECT-ORIENTED PROGRAMMING IN C++

Object-Oriented Programming (OOP) is a powerful paradigm that facilitates the creation of well-organized, modular, and reusable code by modeling the real world using objects, classes, and their interactions. This chapter introduces the core concepts of OOP in C++, highlighting their significance in modern software development.

Introduction to OOP and Its Significance:

Object-Oriented Programming is a programming paradigm that revolves around the concept of objects, which are instances of classes. OOP promotes code organization, reusability, and maintainability by encapsulating data and behavior into objects.

OOP Significance:

- **Modularity**: Code is divided into smaller, self-contained units (objects) that can be developed and tested independently.
- **Reusability**: Classes and objects can be reused in different parts of the program or even in other projects.
- **Abstraction**: Complex real-world entities are represented by classes, abstracting away unnecessary details.
- **Encapsulation**: Data and methods that operate on the data are bundled together within a class, reducing direct access and enhancing data integrity. - **Inheritance**: Classes can inherit properties and behaviors from other classes, promoting code reuse and hierarchy.
- **Polymorphism**: Objects of different classes can be treated as objects of a common base class, allowing flexibility and extensibility.

Classes, Objects, Constructors, and Destructors:

Classes: A class is a blueprint or template for creating objects. It defines the structure, properties (attributes), and behaviors (methods) that objects of that class will possess.

Objects: An object is an instance of a class. It combines data and methods defined in the class, allowing you to interact with it.

Constructors: Constructors are special methods within a class that are used to initialize the object's state when it is created. They have the same name as the class and do not have a return type.

Destructors: Destructors are special methods that are automatically called when an object goes out of scope. They are used to perform cleanup operations before the object is destroyed.

Encapsulation, Inheritance, and Polymorphism:

Encapsulation: Encapsulation refers to the bundling of data and methods that operate on the data into a single unit, the class. Access to the data is controlled by the class methods, enhancing data integrity and security.

Inheritance: Inheritance allows a class (subclass or derived class) to inherit properties and behaviors from another class (superclass or base class). It promotes code reuse and allows the creation of a hierarchy of classes.

Polymorphism: Polymorphism allows objects of different classes to be treated as objects of a common base class. It enables flexibility and extensibility, allowing you to create functions and methods that can work with different types of objects.

Creating and Using Classes with Examples:

Creating a Class:

```
class Circle {
private:
    double radius;

public:
    Circle(double r) : radius(r) {}
    double getArea() { return 3.14159 * radius * radius;
};
```

Creating and Using Objects:

```
int main() {
    Circle c1(5.0);
    Circle c2(3.0);

    double area1 = c1.getArea();
    double area2 = c2.getArea();

    // Use the calculated areas
    return 0;
}
```

Summary:

Object-Oriented Programming (OOP) provides a structured and efficient way to design and implement software using objects, classes, inheritance, and polymorphism. By encapsulating data and behavior within objects, and organizing code hierarchically, OOP promotes reusability, maintainability, and code organization. Understanding OOP concepts is essential for modern software development, enabling you to create robust and scalable applications. In the next chapter, we will dive deeper into the practical implementation of OOP concepts in C++.

PART 2: ADVANCED C++ CONCEPTS

CHAPTER 1: ADVANCED C++ FEATURES

Templates and Namespaces:

- Introduction to templates and their role in creating generic code.
- Exploring function templates and class templates.
- Solving problems with type-independent algorithms.
- Understanding namespaces and avoiding naming conflicts.

Templates:

Introduction and Role:

Templates are a powerful feature in C++ that allow you to create generic code capable of working with various data types. They enable you to write functions and classes that maintain flexibility without duplicating code.

Function Templates:

Function templates allow you to define generic functions that can operate on different data types. You specify a template parameter as a placeholder for the actual type. When the function is used, the template parameter is replaced with the provided type.

```
template <typename T>
T max(T a, T b) {
    return (a > b) ? a : b;
}
```

Class Templates:

Class templates extend the concept of function templates to classes. They let you create classes that can handle multiple data types using template parameters.

```cpp
template <typename T>
class Stack {
private:
    T items[100];
    int top;
public:
    // Class methods here
};
```

Type-Independent Algorithms:

Templates facilitate the creation of algorithms and data structures that are not tied to specific data types. For instance, a sorting algorithm implemented as a function template can sort arrays of various data types without modification.

```cpp
template <typename T>
void bubbleSort(T arr[], int size) {
    // Sorting logic
}
```

Namespaces:

Introduction and Purpose:

Namespaces are a tool to circumvent naming conflicts and organize code. They provide a means to group related code under a common namespace, creating a distinct scope for identifiers. This becomes particularly advantageous in larger codebases or when integrating multiple libraries.

Defining a Namespace:

Namespaces are defined using the `namespace` keyword. All code within a namespace is enclosed within curly braces.

```
namespace Math {
    int add(int a, int b) {
        return a + b;
    }
}
```

Using Namespaces:

To use entities from a namespace, you need to qualify them with the namespace name followed by the scope resolution operator `::`.

```
int result = Math::add(3, 5);
```

Avoiding Naming Conflicts:

Namespaces prevent naming conflicts by providing a separate context for identifiers. If two libraries define functions with the same name, using namespaces allows you to distinguish between them.

```
namespace LibraryA {
    void commonFunction() { /* ... */ }
}

namespace LibraryB {
    void commonFunction() { /* ... */ }
}
```

Nested Namespaces:

You can create nested namespaces to further organize your code and avoid clutter.

```
namespace Application {
    namespace UI {
        // UI-related code here
    }
}
```

Summary:

Templates in C++ empower you to craft generic code adaptable to various data types, eliminating redundant coding. Function templates and class templates are pivotal in creating code that's reusable and adaptable. Namespaces provide a mechanism to dodge naming conflicts, structure code, and establish distinct contexts for identifiers. By employing namespaces, you can adeptly manage code scope and visibility, even in intricate projects involving multiple components and libraries.

Operator Overloading and Friend Functions:

- Overloading operators to work with user-defined types.
- Using friend functions to grant non-member functions access to class private members.
- Implementing custom behavior for operators like `+`, `-`, `<<`, and `>>`.

Operator Overloading:

Overloading Operators for User-Defined Types:

Operator overloading allows you to redefine the behavior of operators when applied to user-defined types (classes or structs). By overloading operators, you can provide custom implementations for operators to work with your own objects.

Implementing Custom Behavior for Operators:

For instance, you can define how the addition operator (`+`) works for instances of a class you've created. This lets you add meaningful behavior to your objects beyond simple arithmetic.

```
class Complex {
private:
    double real;
    double imag;
public:
    Complex(double r, double i) : real(r), imag(i) {}

    // Overloading the + operator
    Complex operator+(const Complex& other) const {
        return Complex(real + other.real, imag + other.imag);
    }
};
```

Usage of Operator Overloading:

With the operator overloaded, you can add instances of your class using the `+` operator just like you would with built-in types:

```
Complex num1(3.0, 4.0);
Complex num2(1.5, 2.5);
Complex result = num1 + num2; // Calls the overloaded + operator
```

Friend Functions:

Granting Access to Private Members:

C++ classes encapsulate their members by default, making private members inaccessible from outside the class. However, sometimes you may need to allow external functions to access private members for specific reasons. This is where friend functions come in.

Using Friend Functions:

A friend function is a non-member function that is granted access to the private members of a class. To declare a function as a friend, you include a `friend` declaration inside the class definition.

```
class MyClass {
private:
    int data;
public:
    MyClass(int d) : data(d) {}

    friend int accessPrivateData(const MyClass& obj);
};

int accessPrivateData(const MyClass& obj) {
    return obj.data; // Accessing private member through friend function
}
```

Custom Behavior with Friend Functions:

You can use friend functions to implement behavior that requires access to private members of a class. This can be particularly useful for operations that don't quite fit as member functions.

Usage of Friend Functions:

In this example, the `accessPrivateData` friend function is used to access the private `data` member of `MyClass`:

```
int main() {
    MyClass obj(42);
    int value = accessPrivateData(obj); // Calls the friend function
    return 0;
}
```

Summary:

Operator overloading enables you to redefine how operators work with user-defined types, providing custom behavior and making your classes more intuitive to use. Friend functions grant access to private members of a class, allowing external functions to work with private data when necessary. Both operator overloading and friend functions contribute to the flexibility and extensibility of C++ classes, enhancing code clarity and usability.

CHAPTER 2: EXCEPTION HANDLING:

- Handling runtime errors gracefully using try-catch blocks.
- Throwing and catching exceptions.
- Creating custom exception classes for specific error scenarios. - Writing robust code with proper error handling.

Handling Runtime Errors with try-catch Blocks:

Introduction:

Exception handling is a mechanism that allows you to gracefully manage runtime errors and unexpected situations in your code. Instead of abruptly terminating the program, you can catch and handle exceptions, ensuring that the program continues to execute sensibly.

Using try-catch Blocks:

```
try {
    // Code that might throw an exception
}
catch (ExceptionType1& ex1) {
    // Handle exception of type ExceptionType1
}
catch (ExceptionType2& ex2) {
    // Handle exception of type ExceptionType2
}
// ...
```

Throwing and Catching Exceptions:

Throwing Exceptions:

Exceptions can be thrown using the `throw` keyword followed by an exception object. This triggers the search for a corresponding `catch` block.

```
void divide(int numerator, int denominator) {
    if (denominator == 0) {
        throw std::runtime_error("Division by zero");
    }
    // Perform division
}
```

Catching Exceptions:

The `catch` blocks are evaluated in the order they appear. The first matching `catch` block is executed. If no matching `catch` block is found, the program terminates.

```
try {
    divide(10, 0);
}
catch (const std::runtime_error& ex) {
    std::cerr << "Error: " << ex.what() << std::endl;
}
```

Creating Custom Exception Classes:

Defining Custom Exceptions:

You may define your own exception classes by inheriting from the standard `std::exception` class or its derived classes. This allows you to create specific exception types that capture unique error scenarios.

```
class MyException : public std::exception {
public:
    const char* what() const noexcept override {
        return "My custom exception";
    }
};
```

Using Custom Exceptions:

You can throw and catch custom exception classes in the same way as standard exceptions.

```
try {
    throw MyException();
}
catch (const MyException& ex) {
    std::cerr << "Custom Exception: " << ex.what() << std::endl;
}
```

Writing Robust Code with Proper Error Handling:

Benefits of Exception Handling:

Exception handling allows you to create robust programs that gracefully handle unexpected situations. It separates error handling from the main logic, enhancing code clarity.

Best Practices:

- Catch specific exceptions rather than using a catch-all approach.
- Use exception hierarchy for different error scenarios.
- Provide meaningful error messages in exception classes' `what()` methods. - Avoid catching exceptions you cannot handle effectively.

Summary:

Exception handling in C++ enables you to manage runtime errors gracefully, avoiding abrupt program termination. By enclosing code in `try` blocks and handling exceptions in corresponding `catch` blocks, you can ensure that your program continues executing sensibly. Throwing exceptions using the `throw` keyword and creating custom exception classes allow you to handle specific error scenarios and create robust code. Exception handling enhances the reliability of your programs and promotes clean separation between error-handling logic and main code.

File Input/Output and Stream Manipulation:

- Using file streams to read and write data to files.
- Formatting and manipulating input/output streams.
- Reading and writing structured data using formatted I/O. - Ensuring proper file handling and resource management.

Using File Streams to Read and Write Data:

File Streams:

C++ provides the `<fstream>` library for working with files. File streams (`ifstream` for input and `ofstream` for output) allow you to read and write data to files.

Opening and Closing Files:

You use the `open()` method to associate a file with a file stream. After you're done, close the file with the `close()` method.

```
#include <fstream>

int main() {
    std::ofstream outputFile;
    outputFile.open("output.txt");

    // Write data to outputFile

    outputFile.close();
    return 0;
}
```

Formatting and Manipulating Input/Output Streams:

Stream Manipulation:

The `<iomanip>` library provides tools for formatting output streams, like setting field width, precision, and alignment.

```
#include <iostream>
#include <iomanip>

int main() {
    double num = 3.14159;
    std::cout << std::fixed << std::setprecision(2) << num; // Outputs: 3.14
    return 0;
}
```

Reading and Writing Structured Data Using Formatted I/O:

Formatted Output:

You can use stream insertion (`<<`) to output structured data, like variables and text, to a file.

```cpp
#include <iostream>
#include <fstream>

int main() {
    std::ofstream outputFile;
    outputFile.open("data.txt");

    int age = 25;
    outputFile << "My age is: " << age;

    outputFile.close();
    return 0;
}
```

Formatted Input:

You can use stream extraction (`>>`) to read structured data from a file.

```cpp
#include <iostream>
#include <fstream>

int main() {
    std::ifstream inputFile;
    inputFile.open("data.txt");

    int age;
    inputFile >> age; // Reads the age from the file

    inputFile.close();
    return 0;
}
```

Ensuring Proper File Handling and Resource Management:

Error Handling:

Check for errors when opening, reading, or writing files using the `.fail()` or `.good()` methods.

```
std::ifstream inputFile;
inputFile.open("data.txt");

if (inputFile.fail()) {
    // Handle error
}
```

Resource Management:

Make use of RAII (Resource Acquisition Is Initialization) principles. This ensures that resources, like file streams, are properly managed and released when they go out of scope.

```
void writeToFile() {
    std::ofstream outputFile("data.txt");

    if (!outputFile.fail()) {
        // Write data
    }
} // outputFile is automatically closed here
```

Summary:

File Input/Output and Stream Manipulation in C++ are essential for working with files and formatted data. File streams (`ifstream` and `ofstream`) enable reading and writing data to files. Stream manipulation allows formatting and aligning output. Formatted I/O allows structured data to be read from and written to files. Ensuring proper file handling and resource management guarantees a reliable and efficient file operation process in your C++ programs.

CHAPTER 3: C++ APPLICATIONS AND PROJECTS

Real-World Applications:

- Exploring diverse fields where C++ is applied, including game development, system programming, scientific computing, and more. - Understanding how C++ contributes to high-performance applications and software libraries.

Exploring Diverse Fields Where C++ is Applied:

Game Development:

Many game engines, including Unreal Engine and Unity (for certain components), are written in or support C++. It allows developers to create complex and visually stunning games.

System Programming:

Operating systems like Windows, macOS, and Linux are often written in C or C++, as these languages provide low-level access to hardware and memory. System programming involves tasks like writing device drivers, managing memory, and handling hardware interfaces.

Scientific Computing:

C++ is used in scientific computing for its performance and numerical computing capabilities. Libraries like Eigen and Armadillo provide linear algebra operations essential for simulations, data analysis, and scientific research.

High-Performance Applications:

C++ is well-suited for applications that require speed and efficiency. Financial software, simulations, real-time rendering, and image/video processing applications benefit from C++'s performance optimizations.

Embedded Systems:

C++ is employed in embedded systems, where resource constraints and

real-time requirements are critical. It's used in devices like microcontrollers, medical equipment, automotive systems, and IoT devices.

Networking and Telecommunications:

Network applications, routers, switches, and telecommunication equipment benefit from C++'s ability to handle data processing and network protocols efficiently.

Understanding How C++ Contributes to High-Performance Applications and Software Libraries:

Control Over Hardware:

C++ provides fine-grained control over hardware resources, memory management, and low-level operations. This control is essential for applications that require optimized performance and resource utilization.

Efficiency and Performance:

C++ compiles to machine code, resulting in efficient and high-performing applications. C++ code can be optimized to execute faster than code written in interpreted languages.

Software Libraries:

C++ has a rich ecosystem of libraries and frameworks that cater to various needs. Boost, for instance, provides a collection of high-quality, peerreviewed libraries covering a wide range of functionalities.

Cross-Platform Development:

C++'s portability allows developers to write code that works across multiple platforms with minimal modifications. This is crucial for applications that need to run on different operating systems.

Legacy Systems and Interoperability:

Many legacy systems are written in C or C++. C++ allows for interoperability with these systems by providing mechanisms to call C functions from C++ code and vice versa.

Summary:

C++ finds applications in diverse fields such as game development, system programming, scientific computing, and more. Its performance, efficiency, and control over hardware make it suitable for high-performance applications. C++ contributes to creating powerful software libraries that solve complex problems efficiently. Its flexibility in cross-platform development and interoperability makes it a versatile language in a wide range of industries and use cases.

CHAPTER 4: USES & PROJECT IDEAS

Project Ideas:

- Creating a Simple Game: Develop a basic game using C++ and explore concepts like user input, graphics, and game logic.
- Text-Based Application: Design a text-based program, such as a task manager or a contact book, utilizing various C++ features. - Discussing the importance of planning, designing, and breaking down projects.

Creating a Simple Game:

Concept:

Develop a basic game using C++. This could be a text-based game or a simple graphical game using libraries like SFML or SDL. Choose a game genre that interests you, such as a puzzle game, a platformer, or a guessing game.

Key Learning Points:

- Handling user input for game controls.
- Implementing game logic and mechanics.
- Managing game states (e.g., main menu, gameplay, game over). - Displaying graphics, animations, and sound effects.

Text-Based Application:

Concept:

Design and build a text-based application that serves a practical purpose. For instance, create a task manager, a contact book, a simple calculator, or a note-taking app.

Key Learning Points:

- Implementing data structures (arrays, linked lists) to manage information.
- Reading and writing data to files for data persistence.
- Using user-friendly menus and prompts.
- Implementing basic search, add, update, and delete functionalities.

Importance of Planning, Designing, and Breaking Down Projects:

Planning:

- Clearly define the project's scope and objectives.
- Break down the project into manageable tasks and subtasks.

- Set a timeline and allocate resources accordingly.
- Identify potential challenges and plan for contingencies.

Designing:

- Create a design document outlining the project's architecture, components, and interactions.
- Decide on the user interface, data structures, and algorithms.
- Plan the software's organization and modularity for maintainability.

Breaking Down Projects:

- Divide the project into smaller tasks that can be completed in a reasonable time frame.
- Prioritize tasks based on their dependencies and impact on the project's progress.
- Assign tasks to team members (if applicable) or allocate time for selfpaced work.
- Regularly review progress, adjust timelines, and update tasks if needed.

Summary:

Creating a simple game or a text-based application in C++ allows you to apply your skills and gain hands-on experience. These projects help you understand user interaction, data management, and program structure. Additionally, emphasizing the importance of planning, designing, and breaking down projects ensures that you approach coding tasks systematically and efficiently. These practices contribute to successful project completion and the development of robust, well-organized code.

Encouraging Continuous Learning and Further Resources: - Emphasizing the value of ongoing learning and staying updated with C++ advancements.

- Providing resources for further exploration, such as online tutorials, forums, books, and coding challenges.
- Encouraging readers to experiment with C++ and tackle more complex projects as they become more comfortable with the language.

Emphasizing the Value of Ongoing Learning:

Staying Updated:

C++ is a dynamic language with ongoing advancements and updates. Stay informed about new language features, best practices, and programming paradigms.

Improving Skills:

Continuous learning helps programmers refine their skills and stay competitive in the rapidly evolving tech industry.

Remaining Curious:

Maintain curiosity about new technologies and to explore how C++ can be used in different domains.

Providing Resources for Further Exploration:

Online Tutorials and Courses:

There are reputable websites, platforms, and courses that offer tutorials, lectures, and interactive learning experiences for various C++ topics.

Websites and Platforms:

1. **cplusplus.com:** Offers comprehensive C++ tutorials, reference materials, and a forum for asking questions.
2. **LearnCpp:** Provides free C++ tutorials that cover topics from beginner to advanced levels.
3. **GeeksforGeeks:** Offers a wide range of C++ tutorials and practice problems.
4. **Coursera:** Hosts C++ courses from universities and institutions, such as

"C++ For C Programmers" and "Object-Oriented Data Structures in

C++."

5. **Udemy:** Features numerous C++ courses with varying levels of complexity, like "Beginning C++ Programming - From Beginner to Beyond."

Interactive Learning and Coding Challenges:

1. **HackerRank**: Offers C++ coding challenges and tutorials to practice algorithmic problem-solving skills.
2. **LeetCode:** Provides a platform for practicing coding skills, including C++, with a focus on technical interview preparation.
3. **Codecademy:** Offers an interactive C++ course for beginners, providing hands-on coding experience.
4. **Exercism:** Provides coding exercises and mentorship in various programming languages, including C++.
5. **Project Euler**: Offers a series of challenging computational problems meant to be solved with programming.

YouTube Channels:

1. **TheCherno**: Offers in-depth tutorials on game development using C++ and various libraries.
2. **Caleb Curry:** Provides tutorials on C++ concepts and programming techniques.
3. **Bucky Roberts - thenewboston:** Offers a series of beginner-friendly C++ tutorials.
4. **CodeBeauty:** Focuses on C++ programming tutorials and real-world examples.
5. **Academind**: Provides tutorials on C++ and other programming topics.

Online Courses:

1. **C++ Programming for Absolute Beginners** - Udemy: Covers C++ fundamentals for beginners.
2. **C++ Nanodegree - Udacity**: A comprehensive program covering C++ programming and concepts.
3. **C++ for C Programmers - Coursera**: A course designed for programmers transitioning from C to C++.
4. **C++ Essential Training - LinkedIn Learning:** Provides a comprehensive overview of C++ basics and more advanced topics.

Remember to explore these resources to find the ones that best suit your learning style and goals. The combination of tutorials, practice, interactive learning, and real-world projects will help you grasp C++ concepts effectively.

Programming Forums and Communities:

Here are online communities where you can ask questions, share knowledge, and learn from experienced programmers.

1. **Stack Overflow:** One of the largest and most popular programming Q&A communities. You can find answers to a wide range of C++ questions and ask your own.
2. **Reddit - r/cpp: A subreddit dedicated to C++** programming discussions, questions, and sharing resources.
3. **Cplusplus.com Forum**: The official forum of cplusplus.com, a website with C++ tutorials and reference materials.
4. **CodeProject:** Offers forums for discussing C++ programming and related topics, along with articles and tutorials.
5. **Dev Shed - C and C++ Help:** A community forum for discussing C and C++ programming concepts and troubleshooting.
6. **Gamedev.net - C++ Forum**: If you're interested in game development with C++, this forum provides discussions on game programming techniques and related topics.
7. **CBoard:** A forum focused on C and C++ programming discussions, with sections for both beginners and more advanced topics.
8. **Qt Centre Forum:** If you're working with the Qt framework for C++, this forum is a valuable resource for discussing Qt-related topics and issues.
9. **C++ Forum**: A community-driven forum where programmers of all levels can discuss C++ programming techniques, libraries, and tools.
10. **Xojo Forum -** C++ Channel: If you're using the Xojo development environment, this forum has a dedicated C++ channel for discussing C++ programming topics.

Remember that when participating in forums, it's essential to be respectful and adhere to the community guidelines. Asking clear and well-formulated questions will increase the likelihood of receiving helpful responses. Similarly, contributing answers and sharing your knowledge can help others and enhance your own understanding of C++ programming.

Books and Documentation:

Here are some highly recommended books for both beginners and more advanced learners looking to learn C++ in depth:

For Beginners:

1. **"C++ Primer"** by Stanley B. Lippman, Josée Lajoie, and Barbara E. Moo:

This book is widely regarded as a comprehensive introduction to C++. It covers the basics, syntax, and programming techniques, making it a great starting point.

2. **"Accelerated C++"** by Andrew Koenig and Barbara E. Moo:

Geared towards beginners, this book focuses on teaching you the essentials of C++ programming efficiently. It's especially suitable for those new to programming.

3. "Programming: Principles and Practice Using C++" by Bjarne

Stroustrup:

Written by the creator of C++, this book offers a gentle and practical introduction to programming using C++. It's ideal for learners who want to build a solid foundation.

For More Advanced Learners:

1. “Effective C++" Series by Scott Meyers:

This series of books (e.g., "Effective C++, More Effective C++, Effective Modern C++") provides insights into best practices, coding techniques, and modern C++ features. They are valuable for intermediate to advanced learners.

2. “C++ Concurrency in Action" by Anthony Williams:

For those interested in concurrent programming and multithreading in C++, this book offers a comprehensive guide to writing robust and efficient concurrent code.

3. “The C++ Programming Language by Bjarne Stroustrup:**

Often referred to as the "C++ bible," this book goes deep into C++ concepts, syntax, and features. It's suitable for learners who want a thorough understanding of the language.

4. **Modern Effective C++"** Series by Scott Meyers:

Building upon his previous work, Scott Meyers' modern series ("Effective Modern C++, More Effective Modern C++") covers the latest features and best practices in modern C++ programming.

5. **"C++ Templates: The Complete Guide"** by David Vandevoorde and Nicolai M. Josuttis:

This book explores C++ templates in-depth, from the basics to advanced template metaprogramming. It's a valuable resource for mastering one of the more complex aspects of C++.

Remember that the best book for you depends on your current skill level and learning preferences. Consider starting with a book that aligns with your knowledge and gradually move to more advanced resources as you become more comfortable with C++.

Coding Challenges and Practice Platforms:

Here are some platforms that offer coding challenges and projects to help you practice and improve your C++ skills:

1. **LeetCode**: LeetCode offers a vast collection of coding challenges that cover various difficulty levels and topics. It's a great platform for practicing problem-solving skills and preparing for technical interviews.
2. **HackerRank**: HackerRank provides a wide range of programming challenges in C++, including algorithms, data structures, artificial intelligence, and more. It also hosts contests and competitions.
3. **Codeforces**: This platform hosts regular competitive programming contests and also has a practice section with a variety of algorithmic challenges that you can solve using C++.
4. **Exercism**: Exercism offers practice problems and mentoring in multiple programming languages, including C++. It focuses on improving your coding skills through iterative feedback.
5. **Codewars**: Codewars presents coding challenges as "kata" that you can solve using C++. You can also compare your solutions with others and learn from different approaches.
6. **Project Euler:** Project Euler offers mathematical challenges that require creative problem-solving and coding. It's an excellent platform to challenge your programming skills.
7. **TopCoder**: While primarily known for its competitive programming contests, TopCoder also provides practice problems and tutorials to help you improve your coding skills.
8. **UVa Online Judge:** UVa Online Judge offers a large collection of algorithmic problems that you can solve using C++. It's a classic platform for honing your competitive programming skills.
9. **Sphere Online Judge (SPOJ):** SPOJ features a wide range of

algorithmic challenges with varying difficulty levels, making it a great place to practice your problem-solving abilities.

10. **CodeChef**: CodeChef hosts monthly coding contests and also offers a practice section with problems categorized by difficulty and topic.

These platforms offer a mix of coding challenges, algorithmic problems, and real-world projects to help you practice and apply your C++ skills. Engaging with these challenges can boost your problem-solving abilities and deepen your understanding of programming concepts.

CHAPTER 5: ENCOURAGING EXPERIMENTATION AND COMPLEXITY:

Hands-On Approach:

Here's some encouragement to inspire readers to apply what they've learned through personal projects, experiments, and coding challenges:

Embrace Practical Application:

By applying what you've learned in C++ through personal projects, experiments, and coding challenges, you take theory and transform it into practical skills. This hands-on experience is invaluable for cementing your understanding and becoming a proficient programmer.

Benefits of Personal Projects:

1. **Real-World Experience:** Personal projects provide a real-world context for applying C++ concepts. This experience is essential for transitioning from learning syntax to building functional programs.
2. **Creativity and Innovation:** With personal projects, you have the freedom to explore your interests and come up with creative solutions. This fosters innovation and sparks your curiosity.
3. **Problem-Solving Skills:** Tackling challenges in personal projects hones your problem-solving abilities. It's a chance to encounter and overcome obstacles similar to those you might face in professional projects.

Experiments and Coding Challenges:

1. **Learning by Doing:** Experiments and coding challenges challenge you to think critically and apply concepts actively. They enhance your skills by pushing you out of your comfort zone.
2. **Variety and Diversity:** Experiments and coding challenges cover a range of topics, exposing you to different areas of C++ programming. This breadth of experience strengthens your overall proficiency.
3. **Immediate Feedback:** Many coding challenge platforms offer immediate feedback, allowing you to see how your solutions compare with others. This fosters a growth mindset and encourages improvement.

Continuous Learning and Growth:

Engaging in personal projects, experiments, and coding challenges is a lifelong journey. It's not just about the destination; it's about the process of learning, adapting, and evolving as a programmer.

Start Small, Dream Big:

Begin with small projects and simple coding challenges to build confidence. As you become more comfortable, gradually take on larger projects and more complex challenges. Don't hesitate to dream big and work towards projects that excite you.

Conclusion:

Personal projects, experiments, and coding challenges provide a dynamic learning experience that solidifies your understanding of C++ and programming as a whole. These activities not only showcase your progress but also serve as a testament to your commitment to becoming a skilled and resourceful C++ developer. So, roll up your sleeves, get coding, and watch your skills flourish!

Gradual Complexity:

As readers become more comfortable with C++, encourage them to tackle more complex projects that push their boundaries and help them grow.

Open Source Contributions:

Suggest getting involved in open source projects to learn from experienced developers and contribute to real-world applications.

Summary:

Continuing to learn and grow is crucial in the world of programming, especially with a language as versatile as C++. By emphasizing the importance of ongoing learning, providing diverse resources, and encouraging readers to challenge themselves, you empower them to become proficient C++ developers who can adapt to new technologies and contribute effectively to the programming community.

CHAPTER 6: SUMMARY OF PART 2:

Part 2 of the book, "Advanced C++ Concepts," delved into higher-level C++ features and their applications. Chapter 1 covered key advanced topics like templates, namespaces, operator overloading, exception handling, and file I/O. These concepts enable developers to write more efficient, versatile, and robust code. Chapter 2 explored real-world applications of C++, presenting project ideas that allow readers to apply their skills in practical scenarios. The chapter also emphasized the importance of continuous learning and provides resources to help readers further enhance their C++ proficiency. By mastering these advanced concepts and exploring hands-on projects, readers will be well-equipped to tackle more complex programming challenges using C++.

PART 3: C# BASICS

CHAPTER 1: INTRODUCTION TO C# PROGRAMMING

Welcome to the world of C# programming! In this chapter, we'll embark on a journey to explore the fundamentals of C# and its versatile applications. C# (pronounced "C sharp") is a powerful programming language developed by Microsoft. It's known for its simplicity, modern features, and wide range of uses, making it a popular choice for various development scenarios.

Overview of C# and Its Applications

C# at a Glance:

C# is a statically typed, object-oriented programming language that offers a balance of high-level abstraction and low-level control. It's part of the .NET family of languages and is designed to work seamlessly with the .NET framework. C# enables developers to build robust and efficient software by combining the benefits of managed code with performance optimization.

Applications of C#:

C# finds its use in multiple domains, demonstrating its flexibility and adaptability. Some prominent applications include:

1. **Web Development:** C# is widely used for developing dynamic and interactive web applications using technologies like ASP.NET and ASP.NET Core. It enables the creation of feature-rich websites with serverside processing.
2. **Desktop Applications**: With tools like Windows Presentation Foundation (WPF) and Windows Forms, C# facilitates the development of desktop applications with modern user interfaces and interactive elements. 3. **Game Development:** C# plays a significant role in game development through its integration with game engines like Unity. It empowers game developers to create visually appealing and engaging games for various platforms.
4. **Mobile Apps:** Xamarin, For IOS & Android.
5. **Cloud Services:** C# is used to build cloud applications and services on platforms like Azure, enabling scalable and reliable solutions.

Role in Web Development, Desktop Apps, Game Development

Web Development:

C# serves as a backbone for building dynamic web applications. With ASP.NET and ASP.NET Core, developers can create web solutions with features like user authentication, database connectivity, and real-time updates. The versatility of C# allows developers to craft web apps that cater to various industries, from e-commerce to social networking.

Desktop Applications:

For desktop applications, C# offers powerful frameworks like WPF and Windows Forms. These frameworks facilitate the creation of intuitive user interfaces and seamless interactions. Whether it's a productivity tool, media player, or graphical application, C# empowers developers to deliver software with a polished user experience.

Game Development:

In the realm of game development, C# shines through Unity, a gameengine.

Setting Up the Development Environment

Before we dive into the exciting world of C# programming, let's set up the development environment to get you ready for action. The process involves:

1. **Installing Visual Studio:** Visual Studio is a comprehensive integrated development environment (IDE) for C# development. We'll guide you through installing and configuring Visual Studio to create, edit, and compile your C# programs.
2. **Creating Your First C# Program**: With the environment set up, we'll walk you through creating a basic "Hello, World!" program in C#. This simple exercise will introduce you to the essential components of a C# program.

Stay tuned as we delve deeper into the world of C# programming and unlock its potential for creating powerful applications across various domains.

CHAPTER 2: C# FUNDAMENTALS

Welcome to the heart of C# programming! In this chapter, we'll dive into the fundamental building blocks that form the basis of C# development. We'll explore variables, data types, operators, control structures, methods, parameters, and return values. By the end of this chapter, you'll have a solid grasp of these essential concepts and how they work together to create functional and dynamic C# programs.

Variables, Data Types, and Operators

Variables and Memory:

Variables are placeholders that store data in a computer's memory. They allow us to manipulate and work with data throughout a program's execution.

Data Types:

C# supports various data types, including integers, floating-point numbers, characters, strings, and more. Understanding data types is crucial for managing memory efficiently and performing accurate computations.

Operators:

Operators are symbols that perform operations on variables and values. They cover arithmetic, assignment, comparison, logical, and bitwise operators, showcasing how they help manipulate data effectively.

Control Structures: if Statements, Loops, Switches

if Statements:

The if statement is a cornerstone of decision-making in programming. Use if statements to execute code based on conditions, enabling your program to make intelligent choices.

Loops:

Loops are crucial for executing a block of code repeatedly. Explore the while loop, do-while loop, and for loop, demonstrating how to use them to automate repetitive tasks and iterate through data.

Switch Statements:

Switch statements provide an elegant way to handle multiple conditions. It’s important to know how to use the switch statement and case labels to streamline decision-making processes in your code.

Methods, Parameters, and Return Values

Methods:

Methods (also known as functions) allow you to modularize your code into manageable blocks. Methods tell us how to declare, define, and call methods, improving code organization and reusability.

Parameters:

Parameters allow you to pass values to methods, enabling dynamic behavior. They tell us how to declare and use parameters to make your methods more versatile and adaptable.

Return Values:

Methods can also produce output through return values. It's important to know how to return values from methods and demonstrate and how these values can be utilized in your programs.

By mastering the content in this chapter, you'll acquire the foundational skills necessary to write meaningful C# programs. The ability to work with variables, utilize control structures, create methods, and handle parameters and return values is crucial as you move forward in your C# programming journey.

CHAPTER 3: OBJECT-ORIENTED PROGRAMMING IN C#

Welcome to the fascinating world of Object-Oriented Programming (OOP) in C#! In this chapter, we'll explore the principles of OOP and how they are applied using C#. We'll delve into the core concepts of classes, objects, constructors, properties, inheritance, interfaces, and polymorphism. By the end of this chapter, you'll have a solid foundation in OOP with C# and be equipped to create sophisticated and modular applications.

Principles of OOP with C#

Understanding OOP:

Object-Oriented Programming is a programming paradigm that revolves around organizing code into objects that interact with each other. This approach promotes code reusability, maintainability, and a clearer representation of real-world entities.

Encapsulation:

Encapsulation involves bundling data (attributes) and methods (functions) that operate on the data into a single unit known as a class. This unit is used to hide the internal details of an object from the outside world.

Inheritance:

Inheritance allows a class (subclass/derived class) to inherit the properties and behaviors of another class (base/super class). This promotes code reuse and supports the "is-a" relationship between objects.

Polymorphism:

Polymorphism enables objects of different classes to be treated as objects of a common superclass. This concept facilitates code flexibility and extensibility.

Classes, Objects, Constructors, Properties

Classes and Objects:

Classes are blueprints that define the structure and behavior of objects. Objects are instances of classes that hold data and methods.

Constructors:

Constructors are special methods used to initialize objects when they are created. We'll cover how to define constructors and understand their role in object creation.

Defining Constructors and Their Role in Object Creation

In C#, constructors are special methods within a class that are automatically called when an instance of the class is created. Their main purpose is to initialize the object's attributes or perform any necessary setup for the object to be in a valid state. Constructors play a crucial role in object creation by ensuring that objects start with proper initial values and configurations.

Constructor Syntax

Constructors have the same name as the class and don't have a return type, not even `void`. Here's the basic syntax of a constructor:

```
class ClassName
{
    // Fields (attributes)

    // Constructor
    public ClassName(parameters)
    {
        // Initialization code
    }
}
```

Default Constructor

If you don't provide any constructors in your class, C# automatically generates a default constructor with no parameters. This default constructor initializes attributes to default values (e.g., numeric attributes to 0, string attributes to null).

Parameterized Constructors

You can define multiple constructors with different parameter lists. This allows you to create objects with various initializations based on the provided arguments. For instance:

```
class Person
{
    public string Name;
    public int Age;

    // Parameterized constructor
    public Person(string name, int age)
    {
        Name = name;
        Age = age;
    }
}
```

Constructor Overloading

You can have multiple constructors within the same class, a technique called constructor overloading. This allows you to provide flexibility when creating objects by offering different ways to initialize them.

```
class Rectangle
{
    public int Width;
    public int Height;

    // Parameterized constructor
    public Rectangle(int width, int height)
    {
        Width = width;
        Height = height;
    }

    // Default constructor (overloaded)
    public Rectangle()
    {
        Width = 0;
        Height = 0;
    }
}
```

Role in Object Creation

Constructors are essential because they ensure that objects start in a valid state. When you create an object using the `new` keyword, the constructor associated with that class is automatically called.

Consider a class `Car`:

```
class Car
{
    public string Model;

    public Car(string model)
    {
        Model = model;
    }
}
```

When you create a `Car` object, the constructor initializes its `Model` attribute:

```
Car myCar = new Car("Toyota");
```

Without constructors, you'd have to manually set attributes every time an object is created, increasing the chances of errors and making your code less maintainable.

In summary, constructors in C# are integral to object creation. They ensure that objects start with appropriate initial values, adhere to proper states, and enable you to create instances of your classes efficiently. Whether you use default constructors, parameterized constructors, or constructor overloading, constructors streamline the process of creating objects that are ready for use in your applications.

Properties:

Properties provide controlled access to class attributes. We'll explore how to define properties and their getter and setter methods.

Defining Properties and Their Getter and Setter Methods

In C#, properties provide a way to encapsulate access to class fields (attributes) by defining getter and setter methods. Properties enable controlled access to data, allowing you to maintain data integrity and add logic to attribute access. Let's delve into how to define properties and understand their getter and setter methods.

Property Syntax

Properties are defined within a class just like methods, but they are used to interact with class attributes. The basic syntax for defining a property includes an access modifier, an optional `get` accessor, an optional `set` accessor, and a data type:

```
class ClassName
{
    private dataType attributeName;

    // Property with getter and setter
    accessModifier dataType PropertyName
    {
        get { return attributeName; }
        set { attributeName = value; }
    }
}
```

Getter and Setter Methods

1. Getter (`get`) Method:

The getter method retrieves the value of the associated attribute. It's called when you access the property. It returns the value of the attribute.

2. Setter (`set`) Method:

The setter method sets the value of the associated attribute. It's called when you assign a value to the property. It validates and assigns the value to the attribute.

Benefits of Using Properties

- **Encapsulation**: Properties encapsulate access to attributes, allowing you to control how data is accessed and modified. This protects the internal state of objects.
- **Data Validation**: You can add validation logic within the setter method to ensure that only valid values are assigned to the attribute.

- **Flexibility**: With properties, you can modify the behavior of attribute access without changing the public interface of your class. This promotes maintainability.

Using Properties for Encapsulation

```
class BankAccount
{
    private decimal balance;

    public decimal Balance
    {
        get { return balance; }
        set
        {
            // Validate and set the balance
            if (value >= 0)
            {
                balance = value;
            }
        }
    }
}
```

Automatic Properties

C# offers automatic properties, which streamline the process of creating simple properties. Automatic properties automatically generate the getter and setter methods for you:

```
class Person
{
    public string Name { get; set; }
    public int Age { get; set; }
}
```

Read-Only and Write-Only Properties

You can create read-only properties by omitting the `set` accessor, and write-only properties by omitting the `get` accessor:

```
class Circle
{
        private double radius;

        // Read-only property
        public double Radius
        {
            get { return radius; }
        }

        // Write-only property
        public double Diameter
        {
            set { radius = value / 2; }
        }
}
```

In summary, properties in C# provide a controlled and encapsulated way to access and modify attributes. By defining getter and setter methods, you maintain data integrity and enhance the flexibility and maintainability of your code. Whether you use manual or automatic properties, you're promoting best practices in object-oriented programming and creating more organized and reliable classes. **Inheritance, Interfaces, Polymorphism**

Inheritance:

Inheritance establishes a hierarchy between classes, allowing subclasses to inherit characteristics from their parent classes. Inheritance is a fundamental concept in object-oriented programming that promotes code reuse and extensibility. Let's delve into how inheritance works and how it benefits software development:

How Inheritance Promotes Code Reuse and Extensibility

What is Inheritance?

Inheritance is a mechanism that allows a new class (called a **subclass** or

derived class) to inherit attributes and behaviors from an existing class (called a **base class** or **superclass**). The derived class can then extend or modify the behavior of the base class while inheriting its properties and methods.

Benefits of Inheritance

1. **Code Reuse**: Inheritance enables you to create a new class that reuses the properties and methods of an existing class. You don't have to rewrite or duplicate code; instead, you build upon the existing foundation.
2. **Extensibility**: Inherited classes can add new attributes and methods or override existing ones. This allows you to extend the functionality of a class without modifying its original implementation.

3. **Modularity**: Inheritance supports the creation of a class hierarchy, where related classes share common features. This modular structure makes your codebase easier to manage and understand.

How Inheritance Works

Let's illustrate inheritance with an example:

```
class Animal
{
    public void Eat()
    {
        Console.WriteLine("The animal is eating.");
    }
}

class Cat : Animal
{
    public void Meow()
    {
        Console.WriteLine("The cat says meow.");
    }
}
```

- In this example, `Animal` is the base class, and `Cat` is the derived class. - The `Cat` class **inherits** the `Eat()` method from the `Animal` class. It doesn't need to redefine the `Eat()` method; it can directly use it. - The `Cat` class also introduces a new method, `Meow()`, which is specific to cats.

Overriding and Extending

Derived classes can override (replace) methods of the base class to provide custom implementations:

```
class Dog : Animal
{
    public new void Eat() // Method is overridden
    {
        Console.WriteLine("The dog is eating noisily.")
    }
}
```

- In this case, the `Dog` class overrides the `Eat()` method inherited from the `Animal` class. The new implementation is specific to dogs.

Polymorphism

Inheritance enables polymorphism, where you can treat objects of derived classes as objects of their base class. This allows you to write generic code that can work with different objects interchangeably.

```
Animal myPet = new Cat();
myPet.Eat(); // Calls the Eat() method of Cat
```

Summary

Inheritance is a powerful tool in object-oriented programming that promotes code reuse and extensibility. It allows you to create class hierarchies, build upon existing functionality, and design modular and maintainable code. By inheriting attributes and behaviors, you can efficiently create new classes while leveraging the capabilities of existing ones.

Interfaces:

Interfaces play a significant role in enabling multiple inheritance and supporting design patterns like dependency injection. Let's explore each concept in detail:

Interfaces Enable Multiple Inheritance

What is an Interface?

An interface in C# defines a contract of methods, properties, events, or indexers that a class must implement. It provides a blueprint for a set of behaviors that classes can adopt. Unlike classes, interfaces do not provide implementation; they only define method signatures.

Multiple Inheritance Challenge

In traditional inheritance, a class can only inherit from a single base class. This can become limiting when you want to incorporate behaviors from multiple sources, especially when the sources come from different class hierarchies.

Solution: Interfaces

Interfaces solve the multiple inheritance challenge by allowing a class to implement multiple interfaces. This means a class can adopt behaviors from multiple sources without being constrained to a single base class.

```
interface ICanFly
{
    void Fly();
}

interface ICanSwim
{
    void Swim();
}

class Bird : ICanFly
{
    public void Fly()
    {
        Console.WriteLine("The bird is
flying.");
    }
}

class Duck : ICanFly, ICanSwim
{
    public void Fly()
    {
        Console.WriteLine("The duck is
flying.");
    }

    public void Swim()
    {
        Console.WriteLine("The duck is
swimming.");
    }
}
```

In this example, both `Bird` and `Duck` classes implement interfaces, enabling them to exhibit flying and swimming behaviors independently.

Interfaces Support Design Patterns: Dependency Injection

Dependency Injection (DI)

Dependency Injection is a design pattern that promotes loose coupling and modularity in software. It involves providing the dependencies (collaborating objects) of a class from external sources rather than having the class create them itself.

Role of Interfaces in Dependency Injection

Interfaces are a crucial component of Dependency Injection because they define the contracts between classes. By relying on interfaces instead of concrete classes, you create a separation between the abstraction and its implementation.

In this example, the `CustomerService` class depends on an `ILogger`

```
interface ILogger
{
    void Log(string message);
}

class ConsoleLogger : ILogger
{
    public void Log(string message)
    {
        Console.WriteLine(message);
    }
}

class CustomerService
{
    private readonly ILogger _logger;

    public CustomerService(ILogger
logger)
    {
        _logger = logger;
    }

    public void ProcessOrder()
    {
        // Process order logic
        _logger.Log("Order processed
successfully.");
    }
}
```

interface instead of a concrete logger class. This allows you to inject different logger implementations, like a file logger or a database logger, at runtime without modifying the `CustomerService` class.

Benefits of Interfaces in DI

- **Flexibility**: You can swap implementations without affecting the client code that relies on the interface.
- **Testability**: Mocking or substituting dependencies becomes easier in unit tests.
- **Modularity**: Components are decoupled, making your codebase more maintainable and extensible.

In summary, interfaces enable multiple inheritance by allowing a class to adopt multiple sets of behaviors from various sources. Additionally, interfaces play a pivotal role in Dependency Injection, promoting loose coupling and modularity in your code by allowing classes to rely on abstractions rather than concrete implementations.

Polymorphism in Action:

We'll walk you through practical examples to showcase polymorphism. You'll see how it enables you to write more flexible code and handle various objects seamlessly.

Practical Examples Illustrating Concepts

Creating a Class Hierarchy:

We'll guide you through building a class hierarchy to demonstrate the concept of inheritance. You'll see how subclass-specific behaviors can be added while sharing common attributes and methods.

Let's build a simple class hierarchy to demonstrate the concept of inheritance and how subclass-specific behaviors can be added while sharing common attributes and methods.

Scenario: We'll create a class hierarchy for different types of vehicles, where each vehicle type shares common attributes and methods but also has specific behaviors unique to that type.

Step 1: Define the Base Class

We'll start by defining a base class called `Vehicle`. This class will have common attributes like `Brand` and `Year`, along with a method `Start()` that all vehicles can use.

```
class Vehicle
{
    public string Brand { get; set; }
    public int Year { get; set; }

    public Vehicle(string brand, int year)
    {
        Brand = brand;
        Year = year;
    }

    public void Start()
    {
        Console.WriteLine($"{Brand} is starting.");
    }
}
```

Step 2: Create Subclasses

Next, we'll create two subclasses of `Vehicle` to represent specific types of vehicles: `Car` and `Motorcycle`.

```
class Car : Vehicle
{
    public Car(string brand, int year) : base(brand, year)
    {
    }

    public void OpenTrunk()
    {
        Console.WriteLine($"Opening trunk of {Brand} car.");
    }
}

class Motorcycle : Vehicle
{
    public Motorcycle(string brand, int year) : base(brand, year)
    {
    }

    public void Wheelie()
    {
        Console.WriteLine($"{Brand} motorcycle is doing a wheelie!");
    }
```

Step 3: Using the Class Hierarchy

Now let's create instances of our subclasses and see how they inherit common attributes and methods while also having their own specific behaviors.

```
class Program
{
    static void Main(string[] args)
    {
        Car myCar = new Car("Toyota", 2022);
        Motorcycle myMotorcycle = new Motorcycle("Harley-Davidson", 2021

        myCar.Start();
        myCar.OpenTrunk();

        Console.WriteLine();

        myMotorcycle.Start();
        myMotorcycle.Wheelie();
    }
}
```

Output:

```
Toyota is starting.
Opening trunk of Toyota car.

Harley-Davidson is starting.
Harley-Davidson motorcycle is doing a wheelie!
```

Summary:

In this example, we built a class hierarchy demonstrating the concept of inheritance. The `Vehicle` base class provided common attributes and methods, while the `Car` and `Motorcycle` subclasses inherited those and added their own specific behaviors (`OpenTrunk()` and `Wheelie()`). This showcases how inheritance allows us to reuse and extend code efficiently, creating a structured and maintainable class hierarchy.

Implementing an Interface:

You'll learn how to create an interface and implement it in different classes. This will highlight the power of interfaces in enforcing a common contract.

Scenario: Let's create an interface for different types of electronic devices, such as `Laptop` and `Smartphone`. Each device should be able to `TurnOn()` and `TurnOff()`, but they may have their own specific implementations.

Step 1: Define the Interface

We'll start by defining an interface called `IElectronicDevice` with the methods `TurnOn()` and `TurnOff()`.

```
interface IElectronicDevice
{
    void TurnOn();
    void TurnOff();
}
```

Step 2: Implement the Interface

Next, we'll create classes `Laptop` and `Smartphone` that implement the `IElectronicDevice` interface. Each class will provide its own implementation of the `TurnOn()` and `TurnOff()` methods.

```
class Laptop : IElectronicDevice
{
    public void TurnOn()
    {
        Console.WriteLine("Laptop is booting up.");
    }

    public void TurnOff()
    {
        Console.WriteLine("Laptop is shutting down.");
    }
}

class Smartphone : IElectronicDevice
{
    public void TurnOn()
    {
        Console.WriteLine("Smartphone is powering on.");
    }

    public void TurnOff()
    {
        Console.WriteLine("Smartphone is turning off.");
```

Step 3: Using the Interface

Finally, let's create instances of our `Laptop` and `Smartphone` classes and call the `TurnOn()` and `TurnOff()` methods.

```
class Program
{
    static void Main(string[] args)
    {
        IElectronicDevice myLaptop = new Laptop();
        IElectronicDevice mySmartphone = new Smartphone();

        Console.WriteLine("Using laptop:");
        UseDevice(myLaptop);

        Console.WriteLine("\nUsing smartphone:");
        UseDevice(mySmartphone);
    }

    static void UseDevice(IElectronicDevice device)
    {
        device.TurnOn();
        // Perform some actions
        device.TurnOff();
    }
}
```

Output:

```
Using laptop:
Laptop is booting up.
Laptop is shutting down.

Using smartphone:
Smartphone is powering on.
Smartphone is turning off.
```

Summary:

In this example, we defined an interface `IElectronicDevice` with `TurnOn()` and `TurnOff()` methods and implemented it in the `Laptop` and `Smartphone` classes. By using the interface, we enforced a common contract that both classes must adhere to. This showcases how interfaces ensure that different classes implement the same set of methods, enabling code to work with different objects in a unified way.

Applying Polymorphism:

Through hands-on examples, you'll witness how polymorphism allows you to write generic code that can operate on objects of different classes, enhancing code flexibility.

Polymorphism allows you to write generic code that can operate on objects of different classes that share a common interface or inheritance hierarchy. This enhances code flexibility and promotes the reusability of your codebase. Let's walk through an example to demonstrate this concept.

Scenario: We'll create a simple program that manages various shapes (e.g., circles and rectangles). We'll use polymorphism to operate on these shapes regardless of their specific types.

Step 1: Define the Base Class

Start by defining a base class `Shape` with a common method `CalculateArea()` that will be overridden in subclasses.

```
abstract class Shape
{
    public abstract double CalculateArea();
}
```

Step 2: Implement Subclasses

Create subclasses `Circle` and `Rectangle`, both of which inherit from the `Shape` base class. Override the `CalculateArea()` method in each subclass.

```
    public Circle(double radius)
    {
        Radius = radius;
    }

    public override double
CalculateArea()
    {
        return Math.PI * Radius *
Radius;
    }
}

class Rectangle : Shape
{
    public double Width { get; set; }
    public double Height { get; set; }

    public Rectangle(double width,
double height)
    {
        Width = width;
        Height = height;
    }

    public override double
CalculateArea()
    {
        return Width * Height;
    }
}
```

Step 3: Use Polymorphism

Create a program that operates on shapes using polymorphism. We'll create an array of different shapes and call their `CalculateArea()` method without worrying about their specific types.

```
class Program
{
    static void Main(string[] args)
    {
        Shape[] shapes = new Shape[]
        {
            new Circle(5),
            new Rectangle(3, 4),
            new Circle(7)
        };

        foreach (Shape shape in shapes)
        {
            double area = shape.CalculateArea();
            Console.WriteLine($"Area of the shape: {area}");
        }
    }
}
```

Output:

```
Area of the shape: 78.53981633974483
Area of the shape: 12
Area of the shape: 153.93804002589985
```

CHAPTER 4: PART 3 SUMMARY

In this example, polymorphism allowed us to create generic code that works with different shapes, regardless of their specific types. By utilizing a common base class and overriding methods in subclasses, we were able to operate on a collection of shapes without needing to know their exact types. This demonstrates how polymorphism enhances code flexibility and reusability, allowing you to write more versatile and generic code that can handle a variety of objects.

By mastering the principles of OOP with C# and understanding how to create classes, objects, and interfaces, you'll be well on your way to building modular and maintainable applications. The ability to harness inheritance and polymorphism will empower you to design robust software that adapts to changing requirements.

PART 4: INTERMEDIATE C# PROGRAMMING

CHAPTER 1: INTERMEDIATE C# FEATURES

In this chapter, we'll delve into some intermediate C# features that elevate your programming skills. We'll explore delegates and events, Language Integrated Query (LINQ) for data querying, and best practices for exception handling. These topics will empower you to write more versatile and robust code.

1. Delegates and Events

Delegates

A delegate is a type that represents references to methods. It allows you to treat methods as first-class citizens, making them more flexible and enabling scenarios like callback functions.

```
delegate void CalculationDelegate(int x, int y);
```

Events

Events are a mechanism to notify subscribers when something of interest happens. They are commonly used to implement the Observer design pattern.

```
class TemperatureSensor
{
    public event EventHandler TemperatureChanged;
    public void OnTemperatureChanged()
    {
        TemperatureChanged?.Invoke(this, EventArgs.Empty);
    }
}
```

2. Language Integrated Query (LINQ)

Introduction to LINQ

Language Integrated Query (LINQ) is a powerful feature that allows you to query various data sources using a consistent syntax. LINQ queries are written in a declarative style and work with collections, databases, XML, and more.

```
var evenNumbers = from num in numbers
                  where num % 2 == 0
                  select num;
```

LINQ to Objects

LINQ to Objects enables querying in-memory collections, arrays, and lists.

LINQ to SQL

LINQ to SQL enables querying and modifying data in SQL databases using C# syntax.

3. Exception Handling Best Practices

Try-Catch Blocks

Use try-catch blocks to catch and handle exceptions gracefully, preventing your program from crashing.

```
try
{
    // Code that might throw exceptions
}
catch (Exception ex)
{
    // Handle the exception
}
```

Exception Types

C# provides various exception types, such as `ArgumentException`, `InvalidOperationException`, and more. Choose the appropriate exception type to convey the nature of the error.

Custom Exceptions

Create custom exception classes when the built-in exceptions don't fully describe your application-specific errors.

```
public class MyCustomException : Exception
{
    public MyCustomException(string message) : base(message)
    {
    }
}
```

Exception Handling Best Practices

- **Handle Specific Exceptions:** Catch specific exceptions before catching broader ones to handle them appropriately.
- **Log Exceptions:** Log exceptions to aid in debugging and troubleshooting.
- **Clean Up Resources:** Use `finally` blocks to ensure resources are properly released, even if an exception occurs.

In this chapter, you've explored intermediate C# features that take your programming skills to the next level. Delegates and events allow you to handle dynamic behavior and notifications, LINQ provides powerful querying capabilities, and exception handling best practices ensure your code remains reliable and robust. These concepts will equip you with the tools to write more expressive, efficient, and maintainable C# code.

CHAPTER 2: C# APPLICATIONS AND PROJECTS

In this chapter, we'll explore the practical applications of C# across various domains and suggest project ideas to put your skills into practicc. Whether you're interested in web development, creating Windows applications, or even delving into game development, C# has you covered. Let's dive in!

1. Practical Applications of C#

Web Development

C# is widely used in web development with the ASP.NET framework. You can build dynamic and feature-rich web applications using technologies like ASP.NET Core and Blazor.

Windows Applications

C# is the language of choice for developing Windows applications using

Windows Forms, WPF (Windows Presentation Foundation), and UWP (Universal Windows Platform). These technologies allow you to create desktop applications with rich user interfaces.

Game Development

C# has gained popularity in the game development industry, especially with the Unity game engine. You can create 2D and 3D games for various platforms using the power of C# scripting within Unity.

2. Project Ideas

Web Application

Idea: Develop a task management web application using ASP.NET Core MVC. Users can create, edit, and organize tasks, and the application can provide user authentication and real-time updates.

Benefits: This project allows you to practice web development fundamentals, including handling HTTP requests, working with databases, and creating interactive user interfaces.

Desktop Utility

Idea: Create a password manager desktop application using Windows Forms. The application should securely store passwords, generate strong passwords, and provide password reminders.

Benefits: This project enhances your Windows application development skills and teaches you about data encryption, file I/O, and user interface design.

3. Emphasizing Continuous Learning and Further Resources

As you embark on C# projects and applications, remember that learning is a continuous journey. Stay up to date with the latest advancements in C# and explore advanced topics such as asynchronous programming, design patterns, and dependency injection.

Further Resources

- Online Tutorials: Websites like Microsoft Docs, Codecademy, and Pluralsight offer comprehensive tutorials on C# and related technologies.
- Books: Reputable books like "C# in Depth" by Jon Skeet and "Pro C# 9 with .NET 5" by Andrew Troelsen provide in-depth insights into C# concepts.
- Community Forums: Engage with the C# community on platforms like Stack Overflow and Reddit to ask questions, share knowledge, and learn from others' experiences.
- Coding Challenges: Platforms like LeetCode and HackerRank offer coding challenges to sharpen your problem-solving skills.

CHAPTER 3: SUMMARY OF PART 4

In this chapter, we've explored the practical applications of C# in web development, Windows applications, and game development. We've also provided project ideas to help you apply your skills to real-world scenarios. Remember that C# offers a diverse range of opportunities, and as you work on projects, continuously seek new resources to expand your knowledge and expertise. By combining learning with hands-on experience, you'll become a proficient C# developer capable of building impactful applications and projects.

PART 5: ADVANCED C# CONCEPTS

CHAPTER 1: ADVANCED C# TOPICS

In this chapter, we'll delve into advanced C# topics that elevate your programming skills to a higher level. We'll explore multithreading and asynchronous programming for efficient parallel execution, reflection and attributes for dynamic behaviors, and dive into dependency injection and design patterns for structuring your applications effectively. Let's dive into these topics that will expand your proficiency in C#.

1. Multithreading and Asynchronous Programming

Multithreading

Multithreading enables your application to perform multiple tasks concurrently, improving performance and responsiveness. Be cautious of thread synchronization to avoid race conditions.

```
Thread thread = new Thread(DoWork);
thread.Start();
```

Asynchronous Programming

Asynchronous programming enhances responsiveness by allowing tasks to run without blocking the main thread. Use `async` and `await` keywords for asynchronous operations.

```
public async Task<int> FetchDataAsync()
{
    // Async operation
    await Task.Delay(1000);
    return 42;
}
```

2. Reflection, Attributes, and Custom Attributes

Reflection

Reflection allows you to examine and interact with metadata, types, and objects at runtime. It's powerful for creating dynamic and extensible applications.

```
Type type = typeof(MyClass);
MethodInfo method = type.GetMethod("MyMethod");
```

Attributes

Attributes are metadata that provide information about types, methods, and more. They enable declarative programming and are used for documentation, code analysis, and runtime behavior.

```
[Serializable]
public class MySerializableClass {
```

Custom Attributes

You can create custom attributes to extend metadata with your own information. This is useful for tagging code elements with additional context.

```
[MyCustomAttribute("Important")]
public class MyClass { }
```

3. Dependency Injection and Design Patterns

Dependency Injection

Dependency Injection (DI) promotes loose coupling by providing dependencies to a class from external sources. This enhances testability, modularity, and maintainability.

```
public class CustomerService
{
    private readonly ILogger _logger;

    public CustomerService(ILogger logger)
    {
        _logger = logger;
    }
}
```

Design Patterns

Design patterns are proven solutions to recurring problems in software design. They provide structure and best practices for creating maintainable and scalable applications.

- **Singleton Pattern**: Ensures a class has only one instance and provides a global point of access.
- **Factory Pattern**: Creates objects without specifying the exact class of object that will be created.
- **Observer Pattern**: Defines a dependency between objects so that when one object changes state, all its dependents are notified.

Summary

In this chapter, you've delved into advanced C# topics that will take your programming skills to the next level. Multithreading and asynchronous programming empower your applications for efficiency, while reflection, attributes, and custom attributes bring dynamic behaviors and metadata manipulation. Dependency injection and design patterns offer you tools to structure your applications effectively. By mastering these advanced topics, you'll be equipped to build sophisticated and well-architected C# applications.

CHAPTER 2: C# IN MODERN DEVELOPMENT

In this chapter, we'll explore how C# has evolved to become a versatile and relevant language in modern software development. We'll delve into its role in cloud computing, mobile apps, and microservices. Additionally, we'll discuss cross-platform development with C# and the importance of staying updated with the latest trends and technologies in the C# ecosystem. Let's discover how C# remains at the forefront of modern development practices.

1. Role in Cloud Computing, Mobile Apps, and Microservices

Cloud Computing

C# plays a vital role in cloud computing with the advent of Microsoft Azure. You can build, deploy, and manage cloud applications using C# and Azure services like Azure Functions, Azure App Service, and more.

Mobile Apps

C# is used in mobile app development with Xamarin, a framework that enables you to create cross-platform mobile apps using a single codebase. This allows you to reach both iOS and Android users efficiently.

Microservices

C# is well-suited for building microservices architecture due to its flexibility and robustness. You can create independent, scalable, and loosely coupled microservices using frameworks like ASP.NET Core.

2. Cross-Platform Development with C#

Xamarin

Xamarin allows you to build native mobile applications using C# for iOS, Android, and macOS. This streamlines development and maintenance, reducing overhead.

.NET MAUI

.NET Multi-platform App UI (MAUI) is the evolution of Xamarin.Forms, enabling you to build cross-platform applications with a unified UI framework.

3. Staying Updated with Trends and Technologies

C# Language Versions

Stay informed about the latest C# language versions. Each new version introduces new features and enhancements that can improve your coding efficiency and expressiveness.

Community Engagement

Engage with the C# community through forums, blogs, and social media. Communities provide insights, solutions to problems, and discussions on emerging trends.

Learning Resources

Leverage online courses, tutorials, and documentation to continuously enhance your C# skills. Platforms like Microsoft Learn, Pluralsight, and Udemy offer up-to-date learning materials.

Conferences and Events

Attend C# conferences, workshops, and events to connect with industry experts, learn about emerging technologies, and network with fellow developers.

CHAPTER 3: PART 5 SUMMARY

In this chapter, we've explored how C# remains relevant in modern software development. It plays a crucial role in cloud computing, mobile app development, and microservices architecture. Cross-platform development with Xamarin and .NET MAUI allows you to target multiple platforms with a single codebase. Staying updated with trends and technologies is vital for remaining competitive in the dynamic software development landscape. By leveraging the strengths of C# and embracing new advancements, you can build innovative and impactful applications that cater to the demands of modern development. In this chapter, you've learned about C#'s significance in modern development practices. It plays a pivotal role in cloud computing, mobile apps, and microservices, while also offering cross-platform capabilities. By staying connected with the C# community and being attentive to emerging trends, you're poised to create powerful and forward-looking software solutions.

50 HANDS-ON EXERCISES

Here are 50 hands on exercises- 25 of C++ and 25 C#. At the end of the exercises there is step by step guidance, but try your best to work them out on your own! Another note, the exercises range in difficulty, from simple to extremely complex. Allow them to be more like guides, and if there are problems you cannot tackle, use it as a goal to strive for and more fully understand! Good luck!

25 C++ Exercises:

Exercise 1: Basic C++ Program

Write a C++ program that takes two numbers as input and displays their sum, difference, product, and quotient.

Exercise 2: Object-Oriented Programming

Create a class `Student` with properties like name, age, and grade.

Implement methods to set and display the details of a student object.

Exercise 3: File Handling

Write a program that reads data from a text file containing a list of numbers and calculates their average.

Exercise 4: Templates and Functions

Implement a generic function template that finds the maximum element in an array of any data type.

Exercise 5: Exception Handling

Write a program that takes user input for dividing two numbers and handles exceptions for divide-by-zero and invalid input.

Exercise 6: Linked List Implementation

Implement a singly linked list data structure in C++. Create methods to insert, delete, and display elements in the list.

Exercise 7: Polymorphic Shapes

Create a base class `Shape` with virtual methods to calculate area and perimeter. Derive classes like `Rectangle`, `Circle`, and `Triangle`. Calculate and display area and perimeter for objects of each shape.

Exercise 8: Command Line Calculator

Write a command-line calculator program that accepts mathematical expressions as input and evaluates them using appropriate precedence rules.

Exercise 9: Template Stack

Implement a generic stack using templates in C++. Test the stack with different data types such as integers, doubles, and strings.

Exercise 10: Binary Search Tree

Build a binary search tree (BST) data structure. Implement methods to insert, search, and traverse the BST (in-order, pre-order, and post-order).

Exercise 11: Memory Management Simulation

Simulate memory management by implementing a custom memory allocator. Create methods to allocate and deallocate memory blocks, and handle fragmentation.

Exercise 12: Advanced Polymorphism

Implement a complex hierarchy of geometric shapes. Design a dynamic way to group shapes and calculate the total area of a group. Utilize advanced polymorphism techniques.

Exercise 13: Concurrent Data Structures

Build a thread-safe concurrent hash map in C++. Implement methods for insertion, retrieval, and deletion while handling concurrency issues.

Exercise 14: Garbage Collector

Develop a simple garbage collector for C++ that can track and release memory blocks that are no longer accessible.

Exercise 15: Graph Algorithms

Write a program to find the shortest path between two nodes in a directed or undirected graph using Dijkstra's algorithm.

Exercise 16: Concurrency and Parallelism

Write a program that simulates a multi-threaded environment where multiple threads are concurrently accessing and updating shared resources. Use synchronization techniques to prevent race conditions.

Exercise 17: Custom Smart Pointers

Implement a custom `UniquePtr` and `SharedPtr` class with the appropriate ownership semantics. Handle memory deallocation and reference counting.

Exercise 18: Advanced Data Structures

Create a self-balancing binary search tree (such as AVL tree or Red-Black tree) and implement insertion, deletion, and search operations. Compare the performance with a regular binary search tree.

Exercise 19: Network Chat Application (Advanced)

Extend the network chat application from a previous exercise to support secure communication using encryption and decryption of messages.

Exercise 20: Matrix Operations Library

Design a C++ library that provides various matrix operations such as matrix multiplication, determinant calculation, and eigenvalue computation. Implement efficient algorithms and test the library with large matrices.

Exercise 21: Memory Profiler

Develop a memory profiler tool that analyzes the memory usage of a C++ program. Display memory allocation statistics, identify memory leaks, and suggest optimizations.

Exercise 22: Code Obfuscation

Write a program that takes a C++ source code file as input and obfuscates it to make it harder to read and understand while preserving its functionality.

Exercise 23: Distributed Computing

Build a distributed computing application using C++ and message passing libraries like MPI. Divide a complex task into subtasks and distribute them across multiple nodes for parallel execution.

Exercise 24: Genetic Algorithm Optimization

Implement a genetic algorithm to solve a complex optimization problem. Define appropriate chromosome representations, crossover, mutation, and selection methods.

Exercise 25: Real-Time Graphics Application

Create a real-time graphics application using a graphics library like OpenGL. Implement complex scenes with dynamic lighting, shadows, and particle effects.

These advanced exercises will challenge your programming skills and provide opportunities for deep exploration of C++ concepts. Enjoy the journey of tackling these complex tasks!

25 C# Exercises:

Exercise 1: Simple Web Application

Create a simple ASP.NET Core MVC web application that displays a list of items and allows users to add new items.

Exercise 2: Object-Oriented Programming

Define a base class `Shape` with methods to calculate area and perimeter. Create subclasses like `Circle` and `Rectangle` that inherit from `Shape` and implement their own versions of the methods.

Exercise 3: Asynchronous Programming

Write a C# console application that fetches data from multiple web APIs concurrently using asynchronous programming.

Exercise 4: Dependency Injection

Implement a simple logging service using dependency injection. Create a class that relies on the logging service to output messages.

Exercise 5: Design Patterns

Implement the Singleton design pattern by creating a class that ensures only one instance is ever created, regardless of how many times it's instantiated.

Exercise 6: RESTful API Client

Develop a C# console application that interacts with a public RESTful API. Fetch and display data using HTTP requests and response handling.

Exercise 7: Polymorphic Animals

Create a base class `Animal` with methods like `Speak()` and `Move()`. Derive classes for specific animals like `Dog`, `Cat`, and `Bird`. Implement their unique behaviors.

Exercise 8: File Encryption Utility

Build a C# application that encrypts and decrypts files using a symmetric encryption algorithm like AES. Allow users to provide a password and choose files for encryption.

Exercise 9: Dependency Injection with ASP.NET MVC

Extend a previous ASP.NET MVC web application to utilize dependency injection for services. Use an IoC container like Autofac or Microsoft.Extensions.DependencyInjection.

Exercise 10: Observer Pattern in UI

Create a C# WPF application that demonstrates the Observer pattern. Implement a simple notification system where one component notifies others about state changes.

Exercise 11: Advanced ASP.NET Core Web API

Extend the Web API from a previous exercise to support token-based authentication and authorization using JWT (JSON Web Tokens).

Exercise 12: Complex Design Patterns

Choose a complex design pattern (such as Composite, Interpreter, or Mediator) and implement it in a real-world scenario using C#.

Exercise 13: Parallel Programming

Develop a program that performs parallel processing using the Task Parallel Library (TPL) to process a large dataset efficiently.

Exercise 14: Custom ORM

Build a simple Object-Relational Mapping (ORM) framework that allows developers to map C# objects to database tables and perform basic CRUD operations.

Exercise 15: Machine Learning Integration

Integrate a machine learning model (e.g., TensorFlow or ML.NET) into a C# application to perform a specific task, such as image recognition or sentiment analysis.

Exercise 16: Advanced Dependency Injection

Extend a previous dependency injection project by implementing more advanced features like transient and scoped service lifetimes. Explore aspects like managing service instances.

Exercise 17: Cryptocurrency Blockchain

Develop a simple blockchain for a cryptocurrency using C#. Implement features like mining, transactions, and chain validation.

Exercise 18: Real-Time Data Visualization

Create a real-time data visualization application using a C# framework like LiveCharts. Display dynamic data streams in various chart types.

Exercise 19: Speech Recognition Application

Build a speech recognition application using C# that converts spoken words into text. Utilize libraries like Microsoft's Speech SDK.

Exercise 20: Natural Language Processing

Implement a basic natural language processing (NLP) application in C#. Use libraries like Stanford NLP or SpaCy to perform tasks like sentiment analysis or entity recognition.

Exercise 21: Distributed Systems

Build a distributed computing system using C# that communicates across multiple nodes. Implement message passing, load balancing, and fault tolerance.

Exercise 22: Real-Time Game Development

Develop a real-time game using a game engine like Unity or MonoGame. Implement complex gameplay mechanics, physics, and multiplayer networking.

Exercise 23: Neural Network Implementation

Create a neural network library in C# from scratch. Implement forward and backward propagation, gradient descent, and activation functions.

Exercise 24: High-Performance Computing

Write a C# program that utilizes GPU acceleration using libraries like CUDA or OpenCL for massive parallel processing tasks.

Exercise 25: Advanced IoT Application

Build an Internet of Things (IoT) application using C#. Connect and control multiple IoT devices, process sensor data, and implement real-time monitoring and alerts.

These challenging exercises will push your C# skills to the next level and provide you with opportunities to work on complex and advanced projects. Enjoy the journey of tackling these difficult tasks!

Step by Step Guidance And Solutions

Exercise 1: Basic C++ Program

Write a C++ program that takes two numbers as input and displays their sum, difference, product, and quotient.

Step 1: Set Up Your Development Environment

Before you start coding, ensure that you have a C++ compiler installed on your computer. Popular choices include GCC (GNU Compiler Collection) and Microsoft Visual C++. You can use an Integrated Development Environment (IDE) like Code::Blocks, Visual Studio, or any text editor of your choice.

Step 2: Create a New C++ Source File

Open your preferred text editor or IDE and create a new C++ source file. Save the file with a `.cpp` extension, such as `basic_calculator.cpp`.

Step 3: Include Necessary Headers

In your source file, include the necessary header for input and output operations using the following line:

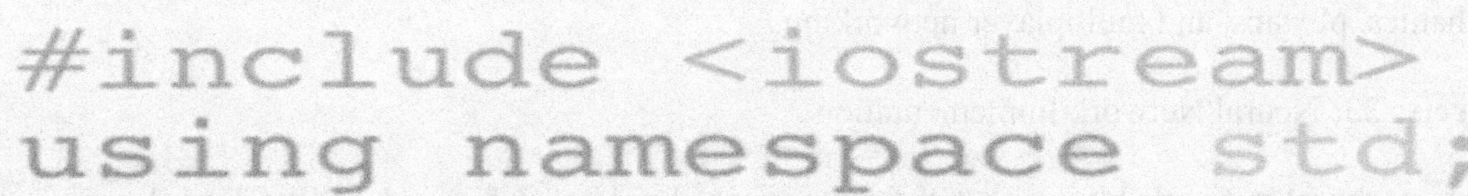

```
#include <iostream>
using namespace std;
```

Step 4: Write the Main Function

Every C++ program begins with a `main` function. Define the `main` function as follows:

```
int main() {
    // Code will go here
    return 0; // Exit the program
}
```

Step 5: Declare Variables

Declare the variables to store the two numbers, as well as the variables to store the sum, difference, product, and quotient:

```
int main() {
    double num1, num2;    // Input numbers
    double sum, diff, prod, quot; // Results
    // Rest of the code
    return 0;
}
```

Step 6: Take User Input

Use the `cin` stream to take input from the user for `num1` and `num2`:

```
int main() {
    double num1, num2;
    double sum, diff, prod, quot;
    cout << "Enter first number: ";
    cin >> num1;
    cout << "Enter second number: ";
    cin >> num2;
    // Rest of the code
    return 0;
}
```

Step 7: Perform Calculations

Calculate the sum, difference, product, and quotient using basic arithmetic operations:

```
int main() {
    double num1, num2;
    double sum, diff, prod, quot;
    cout << "Enter first number: ";
    cin >> num1;
    cout << "Enter second number: ";
    cin >> num2;

    sum = num1 + num2;
    diff = num1 - num2;
    prod = num1 * num2;
    quot = num1 / num2;
    // Rest of the code
    return 0;
}
```

Step 8: Display Results

Use the `cout` stream to display the calculated results:

```
int main() {
    double num1, num2;
    double sum, diff, prod, quot;
    cout << "Enter first number: ";
    cin >> num1;
    cout << "Enter second number: ";
    cin >> num2;

    sum = num1 + num2;
    diff = num1 - num2;
    prod = num1 * num2;
    quot = num1 / num2;

    cout << "Sum: " << sum << endl;
    cout << "Difference: " << diff << endl;
    cout << "Product: " << prod << endl;
    cout << "Quotient: " << quot << endl;

    return 0;
}
```

Step 9: Compile and Run

Save your source file and compile it using your C++ compiler. If you're using the command line, navigate to the directory containing your source file and run the command:

```
g++ -o basic_calculator basic_calculator.cpp
```

Then run the compiled executable:

```
./basic_calculator
```

Step 10: Input and Output

Enter two numbers when prompted and observe the program displaying the sum, difference, product, and quotient of those numbers.

Congratulations! You've successfully created a basic C++ program that performs arithmetic operations on user-input numbers.

Exercise 2: Object-Oriented Programming

Create a class `Student` with properties like name, age, and grade.

Implement methods to set and display the details of a student object.

Step 1: Set Up Your Development Environment

Make sure you have a C++ compiler and a text editor or an Integrated Development Environment (IDE) installed on your computer.

Step 2: Create a New C++ Source File

Open your preferred text editor or IDE and create a new C++ source file. Save the file with a `.cpp` extension, such as `student.cpp`.

Step 3: Define the Student Class

Define the `Student` class with private member variables for name, age, and grade. Declare public member functions to set and display the student's details:

```
class Student {
private:
    std::string name;
    int age;
    char grade;

public:
    void SetDetails(std::string n, int a, char g);
    void DisplayDetails();
};
```

Step 4: Implement the Member Functions

In a separate source file, implement the member functions of the `Student` class:

```
#include <iostream>
#include "student.h" // Include the header file

void Student::SetDetails(std::string n, int a, char g) {
    name = n;
    age = a;
    grade = g;
}

void Student::DisplayDetails() {
    std::cout << "Name: " << name << std::endl;
    std::cout << "Age: " << age << std::endl;
    std::cout << "Grade: " << grade << std::endl;
}
```

Step 5: Create the Main Program

In another source file (such as `main.cpp`), include the header file for the `Student` class and create a `main` function to test the class:

```
#include <iostream>
#include "student.h" // Include the header file

int main() {
    Student student1; // Create an instance of Student

    // Set details using the SetDetails method
    student1.SetDetails("Alice", 18, 'A');

    // Display the details using the DisplayDetails method
    std::cout << "Student Details:" << std::endl;
    student1.DisplayDetails();

    return 0;
}
```

Step 6: Compile and Run

Compile both source files (`student.cpp` and `main.cpp`) using your C++ compiler. If you're using the command line, navigate to the directory containing your source files and run the command:

```
g++ -o student_program student.cpp main.cpp
```

Then run the compiled executable:

```
./student_program
```

Step 7: Observe Output

You should see the program outputting the student's details:

```
Student Details:
Name: Alice
Age: 18
Grade: A
```

Congratulations! You've successfully implemented the `Student` class with methods to set and display student details using object-oriented programming in C++.

Exercise 3: File Handling

Write a program that reads data from a text file containing a list of numbers and calculates their average.

Step 1: Set Up Your Development Environment

Ensure you have a C++ compiler and a text editor or an Integrated Development Environment (IDE) installed on your computer.

Step 2: Create a New C++ Source File

Open your preferred text editor or IDE and create a new C++ source file. Save the file with a `.cpp` extension, such as `average_calculator.cpp`.

Step 3: Include Necessary Headers

Include the necessary header for input and output operations:

```
#include <iostream>
#include <fstream> // For file handling
```

Step 4: Create the Main Program

Write the `main`function to read data from a text file and calculate the average:

```
int main() {
    std::ifstream
inputFile("numbers.txt"); // Open the
file
    double sum = 0.0;
    int count = 0;
    double number;

    if (!inputFile) {
        std::cerr << "Error opening
file." << std::endl;
        return 1;
    }

    while (inputFile >> number) {
        sum += number;
        count++;
    }

    inputFile.close(); // Close the
file

    if (count > 0) {
        double average = sum / count;
        std::cout << "Average: " <<
average << std::endl;
    } else {
        std::cout << "No numbers found
in the file." << std::endl;
    }

    return 0;
}
```

Step 5: Prepare the Input File

Create a text file named `numbers.txt` in the same directory as your source file. Fill the file with a list of numbers, one per line.

For example:

```

10.5

20.7

15.0

```

Step 6: Compile and Run

Compile your source file using your C++ compiler. If you're using the command line, navigate to the directory containing your source file and run the command:

```

g++ -o average_calculator average_calculator.cpp

```

Then run the compiled executable:

```

./average_calculator ```

Step 7: Observe Output

You should see the program outputting the calculated average based on the numbers in the `numbers.txt` file.

Congratulations! You've successfully created a C++ program that reads data from a text file and calculates the average of the numbers.

**Exercise 4:** Templates and Functions

Implement a generic function template that finds the maximum element in an array of any data type.

Step 1: Set Up Your Development Environment
```

Ensure you have a C++ compiler and a text editor or an Integrated Development Environment (IDE) installed on your computer.

Step 2: Create a New C++ Source File

Open your preferred text editor or IDE and create a new C++ source file. Save the file with a `.cpp` extension, such as `max_finder.cpp`.

Step 3: Define the Generic Function Template

Define a generic function template that takes an array and its size as arguments and returns the maximum element:

```
template <typename T>
T FindMax(const T arr[], int size) {
    T maxElement = arr[0];
    for (int i = 1; i < size; ++i) {
        if (arr[i] > maxElement) {
            maxElement = arr[i];
        }
    }
    return maxElement;
}
```

Step 4: Create the Main Program

Write the `main`function to test the `FindMax`function template:

```
int main() {
    int intArray[] = {10, 3, 27, 5, 14};
    double doubleArray[] = {3.14, 1.618, 2.718, 0.577};

    int intMax = FindMax(intArray, 5);
    double doubleMax = FindMax(doubleArray, 4);

    std::cout << "Max integer: " << intMax << std::endl;
    std::cout << "Max double: " << doubleMax << std::endl;

    return 0;
}
```

Step 5: Compile and Run

Compile your source file using your C++ compiler. If you're using the command line, navigate to the directory containing your source file and run the command:

```
g++ -o max_finder max_finder.cpp
```

Then run the compiled executable:

```
./max_finder
```

Step 6: Observe Output

You should see the program outputting the maximum integer and maximum double values from the arrays.

Congratulations! You've successfully created a C++ program that implements a generic function template to find the maximum element in an array of any data type.

Exercise 5: Exception Handling

Write a program that takes user input for dividing two numbers and handles exceptions for divide-by-zero and invalid input.

Step 1: Set Up Your Development Environment

Ensure you have a C++ compiler and a text editor or an Integrated Development Environment (IDE) installed on your computer.

Step 2: Create a New C++ Source File

Open your preferred text editor or IDE and create a new C++ source file. Save the file with a `.cpp` extension, such as `divide_numbers.cpp`.

Step 3: Include Necessary Headers

Include the necessary header for input and output operations:

```cpp
```

#include <iostream>

```

Step 4: Create the Main Program

Write the `main`function to take user input for dividing two numbers and handle exceptions:

```
int main() {
    double numerator, denominator;

    try {
        std::cout << "Enter numerator: ";
        std::cin >> numerator;

        std::cout << "Enter denominator: ";
        std::cin >> denominator;

        if (denominator == 0) {
            throw std::runtime_error("Division by zero is not allowed.");
        }

        double result = numerator / denominator;
        std::cout << "Result: " << result << std::endl;
    } catch (const std::exception& e) {
        std::cerr << "Exception: " << e.what() << std::endl;
    }

    return 0;
}
```

Step 5: Compile and Run

Compile your source file using your C++ compiler. If you're using the command line, navigate to the directory containing your source file and run the command:

```
g++ -o divide_numbers divide_numbers.cpp
```

Then run the compiled executable:

```
./divide_numbers
```

Step 6: Test Exception Handling

Enter various input values for the numerator and denominator, including zero for the denominator. Observe how the program handles exceptions for divide-by-zero and invalid input.
```

Congratulations! You've successfully created a C++ program that takes user input for dividing two numbers and handles exceptions for various scenarios.

Exercise 6: Linked List Implementation

Implement a singly linked list data structure in C++. Create methods to insert, delete, and display elements in the list.

Here's a step-by-step guide to creating a C++ program that implements a singly linked list data structure with methods to insert, delete, and display elements:

Step 1: Set Up Your Development Environment

Ensure you have a C++ compiler and a text editor or an Integrated Development Environment (IDE) installed on your computer.

Step 2: Create a New C++ Source File

Open your preferred text editor or IDE and create a new C++ source file. Save the file with a `.cpp` extension, such as `linked_list.cpp`.

Step 3: Define the Node Structure

Define the structure for a linked list node:

```cpp
struct Node

{ int data;

Node* next;

};
```

Step 4: Create the LinkedList Class

Create a class for the linked list with methods to insert, delete, and display elements:

```
int main() {
    LinkedList list;

    list.insert(10);
    list.insert(20);
    list.insert(30);
    list.insert(40);

    std::cout << "Original list: ";
    list.display();

    list.remove(20);
    list.remove(30);

    std::cout << "List after removals: ";
    list.display();

    return 0;
}
```

Step 5: Implement the Constructor and Methods

Implement the constructor and methods of the `LinkedList` class:

```
LinkedList::LinkedList() {
    head = nullptr;
}

void LinkedList::insert(int value) {
    Node* newNode = new Node;
    newNode->data = value;
    newNode->next = head;
    head = newNode;
}

void LinkedList::remove(int value) {
    if (head == nullptr) {
        return;
    }

    if (head->data == value) {
        Node* temp = head;
        head = head->next;
        delete temp;
        return;
    }

    Node* current = head;
    while (current->next != nullptr &&
current->next->data != value) {
        current = current->next;
    }

    if (current->next != nullptr) {
        Node* temp = current->next;
        current->next = temp->next;
        delete temp;
    }
}

void LinkedList::display() {
    Node* current = head;
    while (current != nullptr) {
        std::cout << current->data <<
" ";
        current = current->next;
    }
    std::cout << std::endl;
}
```

Step 6: Create the Main Program

Write the `main` function to test the `LinkedList` class:

```
int main() {
    LinkedList list;

    list.insert(10);
    list.insert(20);
    list.insert(30);
    list.insert(40);

    std::cout << "Original list: ";
    list.display();

    list.remove(20);
    list.remove(30);

    std::cout << "List after removals: ";
    list.display();

    return 0;
}
```

Step 7: Compile and Run

Compile your source file using your C++ compiler. If you're using the command line, navigate to the directory containing your source file and run the command:

```

g++ -o linked_list linked_list.cpp ```

Then run the compiled executable:

```

./linked_list

```

Step 8: Observe Output

You should see the program outputting the original linked list and the list after removals.

Congratulations! You've successfully created a C++ program that implements a singly linked list data structure with methods to insert, delete, and display elements.

**Exercise 7:** Polymorphic Shapes

Create a base class `Shape` with virtual methods to calculate area and perimeter. Derive classes like `Rectangle`, `Circle`, and `Triangle`. Calculate and display area and perimeter for objects of each shape.
```

Here's a step-by-step guide to creating a C++ program that implements a polymorphic shapes scenario with a base class `Shape` and derived classes `Rectangle`, `Circle`, and `Triangle`:

Step 1: Set Up Your Development Environment

Ensure you have a C++ compiler and a text editor or an Integrated Development Environment (IDE) installed on your computer.

Step 2: Create a New C++ Source File

Open your preferred text editor or IDE and create a new C++ source file. Save the file with a `.cpp` extension, such as `polymorphic_shapes.cpp`.

Step 3: Define the Base Class `Shape`

Define the `Shape` class with virtual methods to calculate the area and perimeter:

```
class Shape {
public:
    virtual double calculateArea() const = 0;
    virtual double calculatePerimeter() const = 0;
};
```

Step 4: Create Derived Classes

Create derived classes `Rectangle`, `Circle`, and `Triangle`, each implementing the virtual methods:

```
    double calculatePerimeter() const override {
        return 2 * 3.14159 * radius;
    }
};

class Triangle : public Shape {
private:
    double sideA, sideB, sideC;

public:
    Triangle(double a, double b, double c) : sideA(a), sideB(b), sideC(c)

    double calculateArea() const override {
        // Calculate area using Heron's formula
        double s = (sideA + sideB + sideC) / 2;
        return sqrt(s * (s - sideA) * (s - sideB) * (s - sideC));
    }

    double calculatePerimeter() const override {
        return sideA + sideB + sideC;
    }
```

```
class Rectangle : public Shape {
private:
    double width;
    double height;

public:
    Rectangle(double w, double h) : width(w), height(h) {}

    double calculateArea() const override {
        return width * height;
    }

    double calculatePerimeter() const override {
        return 2 * (width + height);
    }
};

class Circle : public Shape {
private:
    double radius;

public:
    Circle(double r) : radius(r) {}
```

Step 5: Create the Main Program

Write the `main` function to test the polymorphic shapes:

```
int main() {
    Rectangle rectangle(5, 7);
    Circle circle(4);
    Triangle triangle(3, 4, 5);

    Shape* shapes[] = { &rectangle, &circle, &triangle };

    for (const auto shape : shapes) {
        std::cout << "Area: " << shape->calculateArea() << std::e
        std::cout << "Perimeter: " << shape->calculatePerimeter()
        std::cout << "-----" << std::endl;
    }

    return 0;
}
```

Step 6: Compile and Run

Compile your source file using your C++ compiler. If you're using the command line, navigate to the directory containing your source file and run the command:

```

g++ -o polymorphic_shapes polymorphic_shapes.cpp
```

```

Then run the compiled executable:

```
./polymorphic_shapes
```

Step 7: Observe Output

You should see the program outputting the calculated area and perimeter for objects of each shape.

Congratulations! You've successfully created a C++ program that demonstrates polymorphism using different shapes and their calculations.

**Exercise 8:** Command Line Calculator

Write a command-line calculator program that accepts mathematical expressions as input and evaluates them using appropriate precedence rules.

Here's a step-by-step guide to creating a C++ command-line calculator program that accepts mathematical expressions as input and evaluates them using appropriate precedence rules:

Step 1: Set Up Your Development Environment

Ensure you have a C++ compiler and a text editor or an Integrated Development Environment (IDE) installed on your computer.

Step 2: Create a New C++ Source File

Open your preferred text editor or IDE and create a new C++ source file. Save the file with a `.cpp` extension, such as `calculator.cpp`.

Step 3: Include Necessary Headers

Include the necessary header for input and output operations:
```

```cpp
#include <iostream>
#include <stack>
#include <sstream>
#include <cctype>
#include <cmath>
```

Step 4: Create Helper Functions

Define helper functions to check if a character is an operator and to calculate the result of an operation:

```cpp
bool isOperator(char c) {
    return c == '+' || c == '-' || c == '*' || c == '/';
}

double calculate(double a, double b, char op) {
    switch (op) {
        case '+': return a + b;
        case '-': return a - b;
        case '*': return a * b;
        case '/': return a / b;
        default: return 0.0;
    }
}
```

Step 5: Create the Main Program

Write the `main` function to accept input and evaluate the mathematical expression:

```
int main() {
    std::string expression;
    std::cout << "Enter a mathematical
expression: ";
    std::getline(std::cin,
expression);

    std::stack<double> values;
    std::stack<char> operators;

    std::istringstream
input(expression);
    char current;

    while (input >> current) {
        if (std::isdigit(current)) {
            double value;
            input.putback(current);
            input >> value;
            values.push(value);
        } else if
(isOperator(current)) {
            while (!operators.empty()
&& isOperator(operators.top())) {
                char op =
operators.top();
                operators.pop();
                double b =
values.top();
                values.pop();
                double a =
values.top();
                values.pop();

values.push(calculate(a, b, op));
            }
            operators.push(current);
        }
    }

    while (!operators.empty()) {
        char op = operators.top();
        operators.pop();
        double b = values.top();
        values.pop();
        double a = values.top();
        values.pop();
        values.push(calculate(a, b,
op));
```

Step 6: Compile and Run

Compile your source file using your C++ compiler. If you're using the command line, navigate to the directory containing your source file and run the command:

```
g++ -o calculator calculator.cpp
```

Then run the compiled executable:

```
./calculator
```

Step 7: Enter Expression

Enter a mathematical expression using appropriate operators and operands. For example:

```
Enter a mathematical expression: 3 + 4 * 2 / ( 1 - 5 ) ^ 2
```

Step 8: Observe Output

You should see the program outputting the result of the evaluated expression.

Congratulations! You've successfully created a C++ command-line calculator program that evaluates mathematical expressions using appropriate precedence rules.

Exercise 9: Template Stack

Implement a generic stack using templates in C++. Test the stack with different data types such as integers, doubles, and strings.

Here's a step-by-step guide to creating a C++ program that implements a generic stack using templates and tests it with different data types:

Step 1: Set Up Your Development Environment

Ensure you have a C++ compiler and a text editor or an Integrated Development Environment (IDE) installed on your computer.

Step 2: Create a New C++ Source File

Open your preferred text editor or IDE and create a new C++ source file. Save the file with a `.cpp` extension, such as `template_stack.cpp`.

Step 3: Create the Template Stack Class

Define the template stack class, which will support various data types:

```
template <typename T>
class Stack {
private:
    static const int MAX_SIZE = 100;
    T items[MAX_SIZE];
    int top;

public:
    Stack() : top(-1) {}
    void push(const T& item);
    void pop();
    T& peek();
    bool isEmpty() const;
};
```

Step 4: Implement the Stack Methods Implement the methods of the `Stack` class:

```
template <typename T>
void Stack<T>::push(const T& item) {
    if (top < MAX_SIZE - 1) {
        items[++top] = item;
    }
}

template <typename T>
void Stack<T>::pop() {
    if (top >= 0) {
        --top;
    }
}

template <typename T>
T& Stack<T>::peek() {
    return items[top];
}

template <typename T>
bool Stack<T>::isEmpty() const {
    return top == -1;
```

Step 5: Create the Main Program

Write the `main` function to test the template stack with different data types:

```
int main() {
    Stack<int> intStack;
    intStack.push(10);
    intStack.push(20);
    intStack.push(30);

    while (!intStack.isEmpty()) {
        std::cout << intStack.peek()
<< " ";
        intStack.pop();
    }
    std::cout << std::endl;

    Stack<double> doubleStack;
    doubleStack.push(3.14);
    doubleStack.push(2.718);

    while (!doubleStack.isEmpty()) {
        std::cout <<
doubleStack.peek() << " ";
        doubleStack.pop();
    }
    std::cout << std::endl;

    Stack<std::string> stringStack;
    stringStack.push("Hello");
    stringStack.push("World");

    while (!stringStack.isEmpty()) {
        std::cout <<
stringStack.peek() << " ";
        stringStack.pop();
    }
    std::cout << std::endl;

    return 0;
}
```

`

Step 6: Compile and Run

Compile your source file using your C++ compiler. If you're using the command line, navigate to the directory containing your source file and run the command:

```
g++ -o template_stack template_stack.cpp
```

Then run the compiled executable:

```
./template_stack
```

Step 7: Observe Output

You should see the program outputting the values from each stack of different data types.

Congratulations! You've successfully created a C++ program that implements a generic stack using templates and tested it with different data types.

Exercise 10: Binary Search Tree

Build a binary search tree (BST) data structure. Implement methods to insert, search, and traverse the BST (in-order, pre-order, and post-order).

Here's a step-by-step guide to creating a C++ program that implements a binary search tree (BST) data structure with methods to insert, search, and traverse the tree using in-order, pre-order, and post-order traversal:

Step 1: Set Up Your Development Environment

Ensure you have a C++ compiler and a text editor or an Integrated Development Environment (IDE) installed on your computer.

Step 2: Create a New C++ Source File

Open your preferred text editor or IDE and create a new C++ source file. Save the file with a `.cpp` extension, such as `binary_search_tree.cpp`.

Step 3: Define the TreeNode Structure

Define the structure for a binary tree node:

```
struct TreeNode {
    int data;
    TreeNode* left;
    TreeNode* right;
    TreeNode(int value) : data(value), left(nullptr), right(nullptr) {}
};
```

Step 4: Create the BinarySearchTree Class

Create a class for the binary search tree with methods to insert, search, and traverse the tree:

```
class BinarySearchTree {
private:
    TreeNode* root;

public:
    BinarySearchTree() : root(nullptr) {}
    void insert(int value);
    bool search(int value);
    void inOrderTraversal(TreeNode* node);
    void preOrderTraversal(TreeNode* node);
    void postOrderTraversal(TreeNode* node);
};
```

Step 5: Implement the Methods

Implement the methods of the `BinarySearchTree` class:

```
void BinarySearchTree::insert(int
value) {
    TreeNode* newNode = new
TreeNode(value);
    if (root == nullptr) {
        root = newNode;
        return;
    }

    TreeNode* current = root;
    while (true) {
        if (value < current->data) {
            if (current->left ==
nullptr) {
                current->left =
newNode;
                return;
            }
            current = current->left;
        } else {
            if (current->right ==
nullptr) {
                current->right =
newNode;
                return;
            }
            current = current->right;
        }
    }
}

bool BinarySearchTree::search(int
value) {
    TreeNode* current = root;
    while (current != nullptr) {
        if (value == current->data) {
            return true;
        } else if (value < current-
>data) {
            current = current->left;
        } else {
            current = current->right;
        }
    }
    return false;
}
```

```
value) {
    TreeNode* current = root;
    while (current != nullptr) {
        if (value == current->data
            return true;
        } else if (value < current-
>data) {
            current = current->left;
        } else {
            current = current->right;
        }
    }
    return false;
}

void
BinarySearchTree::inOrderTraversal(Tre
eNode* node) {
    if (node != nullptr) {
        inOrderTraversal(node->left);
        std::cout << node->data << "
";
        inOrderTraversal(node->right);
    }
}

void
BinarySearchTree::preOrderTraversal(Tr
eeNode* node) {
    if (node != nullptr) {
        std::cout << node->data << "
";
        preOrderTraversal(node->left);
        preOrderTraversal(node-
>right);
    }
}

void
BinarySearchTree::postOrderTraversal(T
reeNode* node) {
    if (node != nullptr) {
        postOrderTraversal(node-
>left);
        postOrderTraversal(node-
>right);
        std::cout << node->data << "
";
    }
}
```

Step 6: Create the Main Program

Write the `main`function to test the binary search tree:

```
int main() {
    BinarySearchTree bst;
    bst.insert(50);
    bst.insert(30);
    bst.insert(70);
    bst.insert(20);
    bst.insert(40);
    bst.insert(60);
    bst.insert(80);

    std::cout << "In-order traversal: 
";

bst.inOrderTraversal(bst.getRoot());
    std::cout << std::endl;

    std::cout << "Pre-order traversal: 
";

bst.preOrderTraversal(bst.getRoot());
    std::cout << std::endl;

    std::cout << "Post-order 
traversal: ";

bst.postOrderTraversal(bst.getRoot());
    std::cout << std::endl;

    int searchValue = 60;
    std::cout << "Searching for " << 
searchValue << ": ";
    if (bst.search(searchValue)) {
        std::cout << "Found!" << 
std::endl;
    } else {
        std::cout << "Not found." << 
std::endl;
    }

    return 0;
}
```

Step 7: Compile and Run

Compile your source file using your C++ compiler. If you're using the command line, navigate to the directory containing your source file and run the command:

```
g++ -o binary_search_tree binary_search_tree.cpp
```

Then run the compiled executable:

```
./binary_search_tree
```

Step 8: Observe Output

You should see the program outputting the in-order, pre-order, and postorder traversals of the binary search tree, as well as whether the specified search value was found.

Congratulations! You've successfully created a C++ program that implements a binary search tree (BST) data structure with methods to insert, search, and traverse the tree using different traversal orders.

Exercise 11: Memory Management Simulation

Simulate memory management by implementing a custom memory allocator. Create methods to allocate and deallocate memory blocks, and handle fragmentation.

Here's a step-by-step guide to creating a C++ program that simulates memory management by implementing a custom memory allocator with methods to allocate and deallocate memory blocks, while handling fragmentation:

Step 1: Set Up Your Development Environment

Ensure you have a C++ compiler and a text editor or an Integrated Development Environment (IDE) installed on your computer.

Step 2: Create a New C++ Source File

Open your preferred text editor or IDE and create a new C++ source file. Save the file with a `.cpp` extension, such as `memory_allocator.cpp`.

Step 3: Create the MemoryBlock Structure Define a structure to represent a memory block:

```cpp
struct MemoryBlock { int size; bool isAllocated; MemoryBlock* next;

};
```

Step 4: Create the MemoryAllocator Class

Create a class for the memory allocator with methods to allocate and deallocate memory blocks:

```cpp
class MemoryAllocator {private:
```

MemoryBlock* head;

public:

MemoryAllocator(int totalSize); void allocate(int size); void deallocate(); void displayMemory();

};

```

Step 5: Implement the Methods

Implement the methods of the `MemoryAllocator` class:

```cpp

MemoryAllocator::MemoryAllocator(int totalSize) { head = new MemoryBlock{totalSize, false, nullptr}; }

void MemoryAllocator::allocate(int size) {MemoryBlock* current = head; while (current) {

if (!current->isAllocated && current->size >= size)

{current->isAllocated = true; if (current->size > size) {

MemoryBlock* newBlock = new MemoryBlock{current->size size, false, current->next}; current->size = size; current->next = newBlock;

}

return; }

current = current->next;

}

std::cout << "Memory allocation failed. No suitable block found." << std::endl;

}

void MemoryAllocator::deallocate() {MemoryBlock* current = head; while (current) { if (current->isAllocated) { current->isAllocated =

false;

// Merge adjacent free blocks

```cpp
if (current->next && !current->next->isAllocated)

{current->size += current->next->size; MemoryBlock* temp = current->next; current->next = current->next->next; delete temp;

}

}

current = current->next;

}

}

void MemoryAllocator::displayMemory() {MemoryBlock* current = head;

while (current) { std::cout << "[" << (current->isAllocated ? "X" : " ") << ":" <<

current->size << "] "; current = current->next;

}

std::cout << std::endl;

}
```

Step 6: Create the Main Program

Write the `main`function to test the memory allocator:

```cpp
int main() {

MemoryAllocator allocator(100);

allocator.displayMemory(); allocator.allocate(30); allocator.displayMemory(); allocator.allocate(20); allocator.displayMemory(); allocator.deallocate(); allocator.displayMemory(); allocator.allocate(15); allocator.displayMemory();

return 0;

}
```

Step 7: Compile and Run

Compile your source file using your C++ compiler. If you're using the command line, navigate to the directory containing your source file and run the command:

```
g++ -o memory_allocator memory_allocator.cpp
```

Then run the compiled executable:

```
./memory_allocator
```

Step 8: Observe Output

You should see the program simulating memory allocation and deallocation, as well as displaying the memory blocks and their allocation status.

Congratulations! You've successfully created a C++ program that simulates memory management by implementing a custom memory allocator with methods to allocate and deallocate memory blocks, while handling fragmentation.

Exercise 12: Advanced Polymorphism

Implement a complex hierarchy of geometric shapes. Design a dynamic way to group shapes and calculate the total area of a group. Utilize advanced polymorphism techniques.

Here's a high-level step-by-step guide to implementing advanced polymorphism techniques within a complex hierarchy of geometric shapes in C#:

Step 1: Define Geometric Shape Hierarchy

1. Create an abstract base class `Shape` with virtual methods for calculating area and perimeter.
2. Define concrete derived classes like `Circle`, `Rectangle`, `Triangle`, etc., inheriting from `Shape`.

Step 2: Implement Advanced Polymorphism

1. In the base class, implement advanced polymorphism using interfaces or abstract classes.
2. Design a dynamic grouping mechanism (e.g., a `ShapeGroup` class) to group various shapes together.

Step 3: Implement Group Area Calculation

1. In the `ShapeGroup` class, implement logic to calculate the total area of all shapes in the group.
2. Utilize polymorphism to invoke the `CalculateArea` method for each shape in the group.

Step 4: Compile and Test

1. Build and run your C# console application in your development environment.
2. Create instances of shapes and groups, and calculate their respective areas.

Step 5: Explore Advanced Polymorphism

1. Extend the design to include more complex scenarios, like nested groups or irregular shapes.
2. Experiment with different grouping mechanisms and polymorphic interactions.

Additional Notes:

- Advanced polymorphism can involve interfaces, abstract classes, and intricate object relationships.
- Your implementation can include more advanced techniques like reflection and design patterns.

Remember that this guide provides a high-level overview of implementing advanced polymorphism within a complex hierarchy of geometric shapes in C#. The actual implementation can vary based on your design choices and desired level of complexity.

Exercise 13: Concurrent Data Structures

Build a thread-safe concurrent hash map in C++. Implement methods for insertion, retrieval, and deletion while handling concurrency issues.

Developing a thread-safe concurrent hash map in C++ is a complex task.

Here's a high-level step-by-step guide to get you started with the concepts:

Step 1: Define the Concurrent Hash Map

1. Decide on the basic structure of your concurrent hash map, including the number of buckets and the underlying data structure.
2. Create a class for the concurrent hash map, and define the necessary member variables and methods.

Step 2: Implement Concurrency Control

1. Choose a concurrency control mechanism such as mutexes, read-write locks, or atomic operations.
2. Implement synchronization mechanisms to ensure safe access to the hash map's data.

Step 3: Implement Insertion, Retrieval, and Deletion

1. Implement methods to insert, retrieve, and delete elements from the concurrent hash map.
2. Utilize the chosen concurrency control mechanisms to prevent data races and ensure thread safety.

Step 4: Compile and Test

1. Build and compile your C++ program in your development environment.
2. Create multiple threads that concurrently insert, retrieve, and delete elements from the hash map.

Step 5: Test Concurrency and Performance

1. Test your concurrent hash map implementation with various thread counts and workloads.
2. Measure and analyze the performance, ensuring that concurrent operations are correctly synchronized.

Step 6: Optimize and Refine

1. Profile your code to identify bottlenecks and areas for optimization. 2. Fine-tune your implementation to improve both thread safety and performance.

Additional Notes:

- Developing thread-safe data structures requires a deep understanding of concurrency and synchronization techniques. - Consider using C++11/14/17 features like `std::mutex`, `std::shared_mutex`, and `std::atomic`.

Remember that this guide provides a high-level overview of building a thread-safe concurrent hash map in C++. The actual implementation can be intricate and requires expertise in concurrent programming and data structures.

Exercise 14: Garbage Collector

Develop a simple garbage collector for C++ that can track and release memory blocks that are no longer accessible.

Implementing a garbage collector for C++ is an advanced task. Here's a high-level step-by-step guide to get you started with the concepts:

Step 1: Understand Memory Management

1. Gain a solid understanding of memory allocation and deallocation in C++.
2. Study concepts like reference counting and mark-and-sweep algorithms used in garbage collection.

Step 2: Define Garbage Collector Components

1. Decide on the structure of your garbage collector, including data structures to track memory blocks and their references.
2. Create a class for the garbage collector and define member variables and methods.

Step 3: Implement Reference Counting

1. Implement reference counting for memory blocks using smart pointers or custom reference counters.
2. Track references to each memory block and increase/decrease counts as objects reference or release memory.

Step 4: Implement Garbage Collection Algorithm

1. Choose a garbage collection algorithm like mark-and-sweep.
2. Implement the algorithm to identify memory blocks that are no longer accessible and can be safely released.

Step 5: Integrate with Memory Allocation

1. Overload operators like `new` and `delete` to use your garbage collector. 2. Implement custom memory allocation and deallocation methods that interact with your garbage collector.

Step 6: Compile and Test

1. Build and compile your C++ program in your development environment.
2. Create test cases that allocate and release memory blocks to trigger the garbage collector.

Step 7: Test Garbage Collection Effectiveness

1. Test your garbage collector with different scenarios and memory usage patterns.
2. Monitor memory usage and verify that inaccessible memory blocks are properly collected.

Step 8: Optimize and Refine

1. Profile your code to identify performance bottlenecks and areas for optimization.
2. Fine-tune your garbage collector to improve both memory management and efficiency.

Additional Notes:

- Developing a garbage collector involves deep knowledge of memory management and low-level C++ concepts.
- Advanced garbage collectors might require understanding of memory fragmentation, generational collection, etc.

Remember that this guide provides a high-level overview of building a simple garbage collector for C++. The actual implementation can be intricate and requires expertise in memory management, memory allocation, and low-level programming.

Exercise 15: Graph Algorithms

Write a program to find the shortest path between two nodes in a directed or undirected graph using Dijkstra's algorithm.

Implementing a program to find the shortest path between two nodes in a graph using Dijkstra's algorithm is a challenging task. Here's a high-level step-by-step guide to get you started:

Step 1: Understand Dijkstra's Algorithm

1. Familiarize yourself with Dijkstra's algorithm for finding the shortest path in a graph.
2. Understand the concepts of nodes, edges, and weights associated with edges.

Step 2: Define Graph Data Structure

1. Define a class to represent a graph, including methods to add nodes, edges, and weights.
2. Implement methods to retrieve neighbors of a node and the weight of an edge.

Step 3: Implement Dijkstra's Algorithm

1. Create a method within the graph class to implement Dijkstra's algorithm.
2. Initialize data structures to track distances and visited nodes.
3. Implement the main logic of Dijkstra's algorithm to find the shortest path.

Step 4: Input Graph Data

1. Create a graph object and input the graph's nodes, edges, and weights. 2. Ensure the input data accurately represents the graph you want to analyze.

Step 5: Execute Dijkstra's Algorithm

1. Call the Dijkstra's algorithm method on the graph object, passing the source and destination nodes.
2. Retrieve and display the shortest path and its associated distance.

Step 6: Compile and Test

1. Build and compile your C++ program in your development environment.
2. Test the program with different graphs and nodes to ensure correct results.

Step 7: Optimize and Refine

1. Optimize the data structures and algorithms for performance.
2. Review the code for readability, maintainability, and efficiency.

Additional Notes:

- Dijkstra's algorithm involves concepts of graphs, priority queues, and shortest path calculation.
- Implementing efficient priority queues is important for the algorithm's performance.

Remember that this guide provides a high-level overview of implementing Dijkstra's algorithm to find the shortest path between two nodes in a graph using C++. The actual implementation can be intricate and requires a strong understanding of graph algorithms and data structures.

Exercise 16: Concurrency and Parallelism

Write a program that simulates a multi-threaded environment where multiple threads are concurrently accessing and updating shared resources. Use synchronization techniques to prevent race conditions.

Creating a program that simulates a multi-threaded environment with concurrency and parallelism while handling synchronization is a challenging task. Here's a high-level step-by-step guide to get you started:

Step 1: Understand Concurrency and Synchronization 1. Gain a solid understanding of concurrency, parallelism, and synchronization techniques.

2. Familiarize yourself with concepts like mutexes, semaphores, and thread safety.

Step 2: Define Shared Resources

1. Determine the shared resources that will be accessed by multiple threads. 2. Define data structures to represent these resources and the methods to access/update them.

Step 3: Create Multiple Threads

1. Implement a class or function that creates and manages multiple threads.
2. Utilize threading libraries to create threads and assign tasks to them.

Step 4: Implement Thread Tasks

1. Define tasks that each thread will perform on the shared resources.
2. These tasks should involve reading, updating, or modifying shared data.

Step 5: Implement Synchronization

1. Choose a synchronization mechanism such as mutexes or semaphores. 2. Surround critical sections of code that access shared resources with synchronization primitives.

Step 6: Compile and Test

1. Build and compile your C++ program in your development environment.
2. Run the program and observe the behavior of threads accessing shared resources concurrently.

Step 7: Test Concurrency and Parallelism

1. Test your program with different scenarios and thread counts.
2. Verify that synchronization mechanisms prevent race conditions and data corruption.

Step 8: Optimize and Refine

1. Profile your code to identify potential performance bottlenecks.
2. Optimize synchronization mechanisms and thread management for better efficiency.

Additional Notes:

- Developing concurrent programs requires a deep understanding of synchronization and multi-threading concepts.
- Libraries like C++11/14/17's `std::thread` and synchronization primitives will be useful.

Remember that this guide provides a high-level overview of creating a program that simulates a multi-threaded environment with concurrency and parallelism while handling synchronization in C++. The actual implementation can be intricate and requires expertise in multi-threading, synchronization, and low-level programming.

Exercise 17: Custom Smart Pointers

Implement a custom `UniquePtr` and `SharedPtr` class with the appropriate ownership semantics. Handle memory deallocation and reference counting.

Implementing custom smart pointers with ownership semantics is an advanced task. Here's a high-level step-by-step guide to get you started:

#Step 1: Understand Smart Pointers and Ownership Semantics

1. Gain a solid understanding of smart pointers, their purpose, and the ownership semantics they provide.
2. Study how C++11's `std::unique_ptr` and `std::shared_ptr` work.

Step 2: Define Custom Smart Pointer Classes

1. Create a class for `UniquePtr` that manages ownership of a single object. 2. Implement a class for `SharedPtr` that manages shared ownership using reference counting.

Step 3: Implement Constructor and Destructor

1. Define constructors for both `UniquePtr` and `SharedPtr` to initialize with a raw pointer.
2. Implement destructors to release memory or decrease reference counts as needed.

Step 4: Handle Memory Deallocation

1. In `UniquePtr`, implement memory deallocation in the destructor.
2. In `SharedPtr`, implement reference counting for memory deallocation when reference count becomes zero.

Step 5: Implement Copy and Move Semantics

1. For `UniquePtr`, implement move constructors and move assignment operators.
2. For `SharedPtr`, handle copying by incrementing reference counts and releasing memory when needed.

Step 6: Compile and Test

1. Build and compile your C++ program in your development environment.
2. Test your custom `UniquePtr` and `SharedPtr` with different scenarios to ensure correct memory management.

Step 7: Optimize and Refine

1. Review the code for memory leaks and correctness.
2. Optimize your implementation for performance and efficiency.

Additional Notes:

- Developing custom smart pointers requires a deep understanding of memory management and C++ semantics.
- Consider using RAII (Resource Acquisition Is Initialization) principles.

Remember that this guide provides a high-level overview of implementing custom `UniquePtr` and `SharedPtr` smart pointers with ownership semantics in C++. The actual implementation can be intricate and requires expertise in memory management, C++ language features, and low-level programming.

Exercise 18: Advanced Data Structures

Create a self-balancing binary search tree (such as AVL tree or Red-Black tree) and implement insertion, deletion, and search operations. Compare the performance with a regular binary search tree.

Creating a self-balancing binary search tree and comparing its performance with a regular binary search tree is an advanced task. Here's a high-level step-by-step guide to get you started:

Step 1: Understand Self-Balancing Binary Search Trees

1. Familiarize yourself with self-balancing binary search tree concepts, such as AVL trees or Red-Black trees.
2. Understand how self-balancing mechanisms maintain balanced tree heights.

Step 2: Define Binary Search Tree Data Structure

1. Define a class to represent a binary search tree with methods for insertion, deletion, and search.
2. Implement methods to handle rotations and rebalancing for selfbalancing trees.

Step 3: Implement Self-Balancing Operations

1. Implement self-balancing mechanisms like rotations and color flips for Red-Black trees.
2. Implement AVL tree rotations (single and double rotations) to maintain balance.

Step 4: Implement Insertion, Deletion, and Search

1. Implement insertion operations for both regular and self-balancing trees.
2. Implement deletion operations while ensuring the tree remains balanced.
3. Implement search methods to find elements efficiently.

Step 5: Create Test Cases

1. Create test cases to insert, delete, and search for elements in both regular and self-balancing trees.
2. Measure and compare the performance of both types of trees using various scenarios.

Step 6: Compile and Test

1. Build and compile your C++ program in your development environment.
2. Run the program with different test cases to ensure correct insertion, deletion, and search behavior.

Step 7: Compare Performance

1. Measure the time complexity of operations (insertion, deletion, search) for both regular and self-balancing trees.
2. Analyze the performance results and compare them to evaluate the benefits of self-balancing.

Step 8: Optimize and Refine

1. Review the code for correctness, memory management, and efficiency.
2. Optimize the implementation for better performance and maintainability.

Additional Notes:

- Developing self-balancing binary search trees requires knowledge of tree structures and balancing techniques.
- AVL trees and Red-Black trees have different balancing mechanisms.

Remember that this guide provides a high-level overview of creating a selfbalancing binary search tree and comparing its performance with a regular binary search tree using C++. The actual implementation can be intricate and requires a strong understanding of data structures, algorithms, and lowlevel programming.

Exercise 19: Network Chat Application (Advanced)

Extend the network chat application from a previous exercise to support secure communication using encryption and decryption of messages.

Extending a network chat application to support secure communication using encryption and decryption of messages is an advanced task. Here's a high-level step-by-step guide to get you started:

Step 1: Understand Encryption and Decryption

1. Gain a solid understanding of encryption and decryption techniques, including symmetric and asymmetric encryption.
2. Study cryptographic libraries and algorithms available in C++ for secure communication.

Step 2: Update Network Chat Application

1. Take your existing network chat application and modify it to support encryption and decryption.
2. Integrate a cryptographic library (such as OpenSSL) to handle encryption and decryption operations.

Step 3: Choose Encryption Algorithm

1. Select an encryption algorithm like AES or RSA based on your application's requirements.
2. Implement the chosen encryption algorithm within the application.

Step 4: Implement Encryption and Decryption

1. Modify the sending side of the application to encrypt messages before sending.
2. Modify the receiving side to decrypt messages before displaying them.

Step 5: Exchange Public Keys

1. For asymmetric encryption, implement a mechanism for exchanging public keys between users.
2. Use public keys to encrypt messages that only the recipient can decrypt.

Step 6: Compile and Test

1. Build and compile your C++ program with the cryptographic library integrated.
2. Test the application with encrypted messages and ensure that they can be decrypted correctly.

Step 7: Security Testing

1. Test the application for security vulnerabilities related to encryption and decryption.
2. Verify that messages are properly secured and cannot be easily compromised.

Step 8: Optimize and Refine

1. Review the code for security flaws, correctness, and efficiency.
2. Optimize the implementation for better performance and security.

Additional Notes:

- Implementing secure communication requires a deep understanding of encryption algorithms and network security.
- Using established cryptographic libraries like OpenSSL is recommended for real-world applications.

Remember that this guide provides a high-level overview of extending a network chat application to support secure communication using encryption and decryption in C++. The actual implementation can be intricate and requires expertise in cryptography, network programming, and security considerations.

Exercise 20: Matrix Operations Library

Design a C++ library that provides various matrix operations such as matrix multiplication, determinant calculation, and eigenvalue computation. Implement efficient algorithms and test the library with large matrices.

Designing a C++ library for matrix operations with efficient algorithms is an advanced task. Here's a high-level step-by-step guide to get you started:

Step 1: Define Matrix Class

1. Define a class to represent matrices.
2. Implement methods to initialize matrices, access elements, and perform basic operations.

Step 2: Implement Matrix Operations

1. Choose efficient algorithms for matrix operations like multiplication, determinant calculation, and eigenvalue computation.
2. Implement these algorithms as methods within the matrix class.

Step 3: Optimize Algorithms

1. Optimize matrix operations for performance, considering time and space complexity.
2. Utilize techniques like divide-and-conquer or parallel processing for large matrices.

Step 4: Implement Test Cases

1. Create test cases that involve various matrix operations on matrices of different sizes.
2. Ensure that the library produces correct results and handles edge cases.

Step 5: Compile and Test

1. Build and compile your C++ library in your development environment.
2. Test the library with test cases to verify correctness and efficiency.

Step 6: Test with Large Matrices

1. Test the library with large matrices to evaluate performance and scalability.
2. Measure execution time for complex operations and identify bottlenecks.

Step 7: Optimize and Refine

1. Review the code for correctness, efficiency, and readability.
2. Optimize the implementation for better performance and resource utilization.

Additional Notes:

- Implementing matrix operations efficiently requires knowledge of linear algebra and algorithm design.
- Utilize existing libraries for linear algebra routines to improve performance.

Remember that this guide provides a high-level overview of designing a C++ library for matrix operations with efficient algorithms. The actual implementation can be intricate and requires expertise in linear algebra, algorithm optimization, and low-level programming.

Exercise 21: Memory Profiler

Develop a memory profiler tool that analyzes the memory usage of a C++ program. Display memory allocation statistics, identify memory leaks, and suggest optimizations.

Developing a memory profiler tool that analyzes memory usage of a C++ program is an advanced task. Here's a high-level step-by-step guide to get you started:

Step 1: Understand Memory Profiling

1. Gain a solid understanding of memory profiling, memory leaks, and memory optimization techniques.
2. Study existing memory profiling tools and libraries available in C++.

Step 2: Define Memory Profiler Tool

1. Define a class or tool that tracks memory allocations and deallocations. 2. Implement methods to record memory usage statistics and detect memory leaks.

Step 3: Implement Tracking Mechanism

1. Intercept memory allocation and deallocation calls using hooks or custom allocator.
2. Maintain data structures to track memory allocation sizes, locations, and owners.

Step 4: Memory Allocation Statistics

1. Collect data on memory allocation statistics like total allocated memory, peak usage, etc.
2. Provide methods to retrieve and display these statistics.

Step 5: Memory Leak Detection

1. Implement mechanisms to detect memory leaks by identifying allocated memory not deallocated.
2. Display details about leaked memory blocks and their location.

Step 6: Optimize and Suggest Improvements

1. Analyze memory usage patterns to identify potential optimization opportunities.
2. Suggest improvements like reducing memory fragmentation or optimizing data structures.

Step 7: Compile and Test

1. Build and compile your C++ memory profiler tool.
2. Test the tool with different C++ programs to detect memory leaks and gather statistics.

Step 8: Optimize and Refine

1. Review the code for correctness and efficiency.
2. Optimize the implementation for better performance and accuracy.

Additional Notes:

- Implementing a memory profiler requires knowledge of memory management, C++ internals, and system-level programming. - Use tools like Valgrind or address sanitizers for memory profiling if available.

Remember that this guide provides a high-level overview of developing a memory profiler tool for C++. The actual implementation can be intricate and requires expertise in memory management, C++ internals, and lowlevel programming.

Exercise 22: Code Obfuscation

Write a program that takes a C++ source code file as input and obfuscates it to make it harder to read and understand while preserving its functionality.

Writing a program to obfuscate C++ source code is an advanced task. Here's a high-level step-by-step guide to get you started:

Step 1: Understand Code Obfuscation

1. Gain a solid understanding of code obfuscation techniques.
2. Study common methods used to make code harder to read and understand.

Step 2: Define Obfuscation Program

1. Write a program that reads a C++ source code file as input.
2. Implement methods to obfuscate the code while keeping it functional.

Step 3: Implement Obfuscation Techniques

1. Implement techniques such as renaming variables, functions, and classes with cryptic names.
2. Add unnecessary code structures like extra loops or conditional statements.

Step 4: Preserve Functionality

1. Ensure that the obfuscated code retains its original functionality.
2. Test the obfuscated code with various scenarios to verify correctness.

Step 5: Compile and Test

1. Build and compile your C++ obfuscation program in your development environment.
2. Test the program with different source code files to ensure obfuscation.

Step 6: Optimize and Refine

1. Review the code for correctness and quality of obfuscation.
2. Optimize the obfuscation techniques for better effectiveness.

Step 7: Additional Considerations

1. Keep a backup of the original source code in case you need to revert changes.
2. Understand that obfuscation might impact maintainability and readability.

Additional Notes:

- Code obfuscation aims to make code less readable while maintaining its functionality.
- Obfuscation should not be used to hide malicious code.

Remember that this guide provides a high-level overview of writing a program to obfuscate C++ source code. The actual implementation can be intricate and requires expertise in code transformation techniques and C++ programming.

Exercise 23: Distributed Computing

Build a distributed computing application using C++ and message passing libraries like MPI. Divide a complex task into subtasks and distribute them across multiple nodes for parallel execution.

Building a distributed computing application using C++ and message passing libraries like MPI is an advanced task. Here's a high-level step-bystep guide to get you started:

Step 1: Understand Distributed Computing and MPI

1. Gain a solid understanding of distributed computing concepts, parallel programming, and MPI (Message Passing Interface).
2. Study how MPI enables communication between processes running on different nodes.

Step 2: Define Complex Task and Subtasks

Choose a complex task that can be divided into subtasks.

2. Identify how to divide the task into smaller units that can be executed in parallel.

Step 3: Implement Message Passing

1. Set up an MPI environment on multiple nodes.
2. Implement message passing routines to send and receive data between processes.

Step 4: Distribute Subtasks

1. Divide the complex task's subtasks among the processes.
2. Distribute data and instructions for processing to each process.

Step 5: Parallel Execution

1. Implement each process to independently execute its subtask.
2. Ensure synchronization and coordination among processes as needed.

Step 6: Gather Results

1. Implement a mechanism to collect results from all processes.
2. Aggregate and analyze the results to obtain the final outcome.

Step 7: Compile and Test

1. Build and compile your C++ distributed computing application with the MPI library integrated.
2. Test the application on multiple nodes to ensure proper distribution and parallel execution.

Step 8: Performance Optimization

1. Monitor and optimize communication overhead and load balancing.
2. Evaluate the performance of your application and identify bottlenecks.

Step 9: Optimize and Refine

1. Review the code for correctness, performance, and efficiency.
2. Optimize the implementation for better parallelism and resource utilization.

Additional Notes:

- Developing distributed computing applications requires knowledge of parallel programming, message passing, and system-level concepts. - Use established MPI libraries and consider factors like network latency and node availability.

Remember that this guide provides a high-level overview of building a distributed computing application using C++ and MPI. The actual implementation can be intricate and requires expertise in parallel programming, distributed systems, and low-level programming.

Exercise 24: Genetic Algorithm Optimization

Implement a genetic algorithm to solve a complex optimization problem. Define appropriate chromosome representations, crossover, mutation, and selection methods.

Implementing a genetic algorithm for complex optimization is an advanced task. Here's a high-level step-by-step guide to get you started:

Step 1: Understand Genetic Algorithms

1. Gain a solid understanding of genetic algorithms and their application in optimization.
2. Study the concepts of chromosomes, population, selection, crossover, and mutation.

Step 2: Define Optimization Problem

1. Choose a complex optimization problem that can be solved using a genetic algorithm.
2. Identify the objective function to be minimized or maximized.

Step 3: Chromosome Representation

1. Define a suitable chromosome representation for the problem.
2. Encode problem variables into chromosomes.

Step 4: Initialize Population

1. Generate an initial population of chromosomes randomly or using heuristics.
2. Ensure diversity in the initial population.

Step 5: Selection

1. Implement selection methods like roulette wheel, tournament, or rankbased selection.
2. Choose parents from the population based on their fitness.

Step 6: Crossover

Implement crossover operators to combine genetic information of parents.

2. Choose suitable crossover points based on the chromosome representation.

Step 7: Mutation

1. Implement mutation operators to introduce genetic diversity.
2. Apply mutations to certain chromosomes with a specified probability.

Step 8: Evaluate Fitness

1. Evaluate the fitness of each chromosome based on the objective function.
2. Assign a fitness value to each chromosome.

Step 9: Repeat Generations

1. Iterate through generations of populations using selection, crossover, and mutation.
2. Terminate the algorithm when a stopping criterion is met.

Step 10: Extract Solution

1. Extract the best chromosome from the final population as the solution.
2. Decode the chromosome to obtain the optimized variables.

Step 11: Compile and Test

1. Build and compile your C++ program implementing the genetic algorithm.
2. Test the algorithm on optimization problems with known solutions.

Step 12: Performance Optimization

1. Monitor convergence and diversity of the population.
2. Fine-tune parameters like population size, mutation rate, and selection methods.

Step 13: Optimize and Refine

1. Review the code for correctness and efficiency.
2. Optimize the implementation for better convergence and solution quality.

Additional Notes:

- Implementing a genetic algorithm requires a strong understanding of optimization, algorithm design, and programming.
- Consider using existing libraries for random number generation and fitness evaluation.

Remember that this guide provides a high-level overview of implementing a genetic algorithm for complex optimization using C++. The actual implementation can be intricate and requires expertise in optimization techniques, algorithm design, and programming.

Exercise 25: Real-Time Graphics Application

Create a real-time graphics application using a graphics library like OpenGL. Implement complex scenes with dynamic lighting, shadows, and particle effects.

Creating a real-time graphics application using a graphics library like OpenGL is an advanced task. Here's a high-level step-by-step guide to get you started:

Step 1: Understand Graphics Programming

1. Gain a solid understanding of graphics programming concepts, OpenGL, shaders, and rendering pipelines.
2. Study the basics of 3D rendering, lighting, shadows, and particle effects.

Step 2: Choose a Graphics Library

1. Choose a graphics library like OpenGL that suits your platform and programming language.
2. Set up the development environment with necessary libraries and tools.

Step 3: Define Scene and Objects

1. Define the 3D scene layout and objects to be rendered.
2. Create models for objects with appropriate vertices, textures, and normals.

Step 4: Implement Rendering Pipeline

1. Implement vertex and fragment shaders for rendering objects.
2. Set up the rendering pipeline to process vertices and apply lighting.

Step 5: Dynamic Lighting

1. Implement dynamic lighting techniques like Phong shading or PBR. 2. Introduce point lights, directional lights, and spotlights in the scene.

Step 6: Shadows

Implement shadow mapping techniques for realistic shadow rendering.

2. Apply shadow maps to objects in the scene to simulate shadows.

Step 7: Particle Effects

1. Implement particle systems for effects like fire, smoke, or explosions.
2. Design shaders and update mechanisms for particle animations.

Step 8: User Interaction

1. Implement user interaction for camera movement and scene navigation.
2. Set up input handling for user-controlled actions.

Step 9: Compile and Test

1. Build and compile your real-time graphics application with OpenGL integrated.
2. Test the application with various scenes and lighting setups.

Step 10: Performance Optimization

1. Monitor frame rates and optimize rendering performance.
2. Implement techniques like frustum culling and level of detail (LOD).

Step 11: Fine-Tuning and Enhancements

1. Fine-tune shaders, lighting parameters, and effects for desired visuals.
2. Add post-processing effects like bloom, depth of field, or motion blur.

Step 12: Optimize and Refine

1. Review the code for correctness, performance, and visual quality.
2. Optimize rendering techniques and memory usage.

Additional Notes:

- Creating a real-time graphics application requires expertise in graphics programming, shaders, and mathematics.
- Familiarize yourself with OpenGL documentation and resources.

Remember that this guide provides a high-level overview of creating a realtime graphics application using OpenGL. The actual implementation can be intricate and requires expertise in graphics programming, mathematics, and algorithm design.

C# Exercises

Exercise 1: Simple Web Application

Create a simple ASP.NET Core MVC web application that displays a list of items and allows users to add new items.

Creating a simple ASP.NET Core MVC web application is a great starting point. Here's a step-by-step guide to help you achieve that:

Step 1: Set Up Your Development Environment

1. Install Visual Studio or Visual Studio Code with the ASP.NET Core workload.
2. Ensure you have the .NET Core SDK installed.

Step 2: Create a New ASP.NET Core MVC Project 1. Open Visual Studio or Visual Studio Code.

2. Create a new project using the ASP.NET Core Web Application template with MVC.
3. Choose a project name and location.

Step 3: Define Model

1. Create a model class (e.g., `Item`) with properties like `Id`, `Name`, and `Description`.
2. Add the model class to the `Models`folder.

Step 4: Set Up Controllers

1. Create a controller (e.g., `ItemsController`) using the MVC Controller with Views template.
2. Implement actions for listing items and adding new items.

Step 5: Create Views

1. Add views for listing items and adding new items.
2. Use Razor syntax to display and capture data.

Step 6: Configure Routing

1. Configure routing in the `Startup.cs` file to map URLs to controller actions.

2. Define routes for listing items and adding new items.

Step 7: Implement Data Storage

Set up a simple in-memory data storage (e.g., a list) for storing items.

2. Modify the controller to interact with this data storage.

Step 8: Build and Run

1. Build the project.
2. Run the application to see your simple web application in action.

Step 9: Testing

1. Access the URLs for listing items and adding new items in your browser.
2. Test the functionality of your web application.

Step 10: Enhancements

1. Improve the user interface with CSS styling.
2. Implement editing and deleting functionality for items.
3. Store data persistently using a database.

Step 11: Deployment (Optional)

1. Deploy your web application to a hosting platform or server.
2. Configure your application to run in a production environment.

Additional Notes:

- This guide provides a high-level overview of creating a simple ASP.NET Core MVC web application. For more complex features, refer to official documentation and tutorials.
- Explore ASP.NET Core's features like dependency injection, Razor pages, and data validation.

Remember that creating a web application involves various aspects, including frontend development, backend logic, and user interaction. As you progress, consider referring to official documentation and online resources for detailed implementation steps.

Exercise 2: Object-Oriented Programming

Define a base class `Shape` with methods to calculate area and perimeter. Create subclasses like `Circle` and `Rectangle` that inherit from `Shape` and implement their own versions of the methods.

Creating an object-oriented programming exercise involving base classes and subclasses is a fundamental practice. Here's a step-by-step guide to help you achieve this:

Step 1: Define Base Class `Shape`

1. Create a new C# project in Visual Studio or Visual Studio Code.
2. Define a base class `Shape` with properties or fields for common attributes (e.g., `Width`, `Height`, `Radius`).
3. Implement methods for calculating area and perimeter in the `Shape` class. These methods can be declared as `virtual`.

Step 2: Create Subclasses

1. Create subclasses like `Circle` and `Rectangle`.
2. Inherit from the `Shape` class using the `:` symbol.
3. Implement constructors in the subclasses to initialize specific attributes (e.g., `Radius`for `Circle`, `Width` and `Height` for `Rectangle`).

Step 3: Override Methods

1. In the `Circle` and `Rectangle` subclasses, override the `CalculateArea()` and `CalculatePerimeter()` methods inherited from the base class.
2. Implement the specific formulas for calculating area and perimeter for each shape.

Step 4: Main Program

1. In the `Program.cs` file, create instances of `Circle` and `Rectangle`.
2. Call the `CalculateArea()` and `CalculatePerimeter()` methods on these instances.

Step 5: Build and Run

1. Build the project.
2. Run the application to see the calculated area and perimeter for different shapes.

Step 6: Enhancements

1. Add more subclasses (e.g., `Triangle`, `Square`) and implement their respective methods.
2. Implement error handling for invalid dimensions.

Step 7: Testing

1. Test your code with various dimensions for different shapes.
2. Verify that the calculated area and perimeter are accurate.

Step 8: Documentation (Optional)

1. Add comments and documentation to your code for clarity.
2. Describe the purpose of the base class and its subclasses.

Additional Notes:

- This guide provides a basic implementation of object-oriented programming concepts. As you progress, consider exploring more advanced features like abstract classes, interfaces, and design patterns. - Experiment with additional geometric shapes and their calculations.

Remember that this exercise serves as a starting point to grasp the concepts of inheritance and method overriding in object-oriented programming. You can continue to build on this foundation as you learn more about advanced OOP concepts and design principles.

Exercise 3: Asynchronous Programming

Write a C# console application that fetches data from multiple web APIs concurrently using asynchronous programming.

Creating a C# console application that fetches data from multiple web APIs concurrently using asynchronous programming is a great way to explore asynchronous operations. Here's a step-by-step guide to help you achieve this:

Step 1: Create a New Console Application 1. Open Visual Studio or Visual Studio Code.

2. Create a new console application project.

Step 2: Add Necessary Packages

1. Use NuGet to add the `HttpClient`package to your project for making web requests.
2. Ensure you have the `async` and `await` keywords available in your C# version.

Step 3: Define API Endpoints

1. Choose a few web APIs with different data (e.g., JSON responses).
2. Define the API endpoints you'll be fetching data from.

Step 4: Implement Fetching Logic

1. In the `Program.cs` file, create a method for fetching data asynchronously.
2. Use the `HttpClient` class to make asynchronous requests to the API endpoints.

Step 5: Execute Concurrently

1. In the `Main` method, create tasks for each API request using the `Task.Run` method.
2. Use `Task.WhenAll` to await all tasks concurrently.

Step 6: Process and Display Data

1. Asynchronously process the responses you receive from the API calls.

2. Display the fetched data in the console.

Step 7: Build and Run

1. Build the project.
2. Run the application to see the data fetched from multiple APIs concurrently.

Step 8: Enhancements

1. Implement error handling for failed API requests.
2. Experiment with various APIs and different methods for processing fetched data.

Step 9: Testing

1. Test your application with different APIs and endpoints.
2. Observe how asynchronous programming improves performance.

Additional Notes:

- Asynchronous programming can greatly enhance the efficiency of applications that need to perform multiple operations concurrently. - This guide provides a basic implementation of asynchronous programming in C#. As you progress, consider exploring more advanced topics like cancellation tokens and error handling.

Remember that this exercise aims to introduce you to asynchronous programming in C#. As you become more comfortable with the concept, you can explore more complex scenarios and dive deeper into asynchronous patterns and practices.

Exercise 4: Dependency Injection

Implement a simple logging service using dependency injection. Create a class that relies on the logging service to output messages.

Implementing a simple logging service using dependency injection is a great way to understand the benefits of loose coupling and better code organization. Here's a step-by-step guide to help you achieve this:

Step 1: Create a New Console Application 1. Open Visual Studio or Visual Studio Code.

2. Create a new console application project.

Step 2: Define Logging Service Interface

1. Create an interface named `ILogger` that declares a method like `Log(string message)`.

Step 3: Implement Logging Service

1. Create a class named `ConsoleLogger` that implements the `ILogger` interface.
2. Implement the `Log` method to output messages to the console.

Step 4: Add Dependency Injection

1. In the `Program.cs` file, instantiate an instance of the `ConsoleLogger` class.
2. Create a class that relies on the logging service (e.g., `UserService`).

Step 5: Inject Logging Service

1. Modify the constructor of the class that relies on the logging service to accept an instance of the `ILogger` interface. 2. Store the passed logger instance as a private field.

Step 6: Use Dependency Injection

1. In the `Main` method, create an instance of the class (e.g., `UserService`) and pass the logger instance to its constructor.
2. Use the injected logger to output messages.

Step 7: Build and Run

1. Build the project.
2. Run the application to see the output messages using the injected logging service.

Step 8: Enhancements

1. Experiment with different types of logging services (e.g., file logger, database logger).
2. Explore more advanced dependency injection containers like Autofac or Microsoft.Extensions.DependencyInjection.

Step 9: Testing

1. Test your application by changing the logging service implementation without modifying the classes that depend on it.
2. Observe how dependency injection promotes flexibility and testability.

Additional Notes:

- This guide provides a basic introduction to dependency injection in C#. As you progress, consider exploring more complex scenarios, scopes, and configuration.

Remember that this exercise aims to demonstrate how dependency injection improves code maintainability and testability by allowing components to be loosely coupled. As you delve deeper into dependency injection, you'll find more advanced use cases and patterns to apply in your projects.

Exercise 5: Design Patterns

Implement the Singleton design pattern by creating a class that ensures only one instance is ever created, regardless of how many times it's instantiated.

Implementing the Singleton design pattern is a great way to understand how to ensure that only one instance of a class is created. Here's a step-bystep guide to help you achieve this:

Step 1: Create a New Console Application 1. Open Visual Studio or Visual Studio Code.

2. Create a new console application project.

Step 2: Create Singleton Class

1. Create a class named `Singleton` that will implement the Singleton pattern.
2. Define a private static field to hold the single instance of the class.
3. Make the constructor private to prevent external instantiation.

Step 3: Provide a Static Method

1. Create a public static method within the `Singleton` class to allow access to the single instance.
2. Implement logic to create and return the instance if it doesn't exist, or simply return the existing instance.

Step 4: Build and Run

1. Build the project.
2. In the `Main` method, use the static method of the `Singleton` class to obtain instances and demonstrate that only one instance is created.

Step 5: Enhancements

1. Experiment with multithreading scenarios and ensure thread-safety of your Singleton implementation using locking mechanisms or other synchronization methods.

Step 6: Testing

1. Test your Singleton implementation by creating instances and confirming that they are the same instance.
2. Test the behavior in different parts of your code.

Additional Notes:

- The Singleton pattern ensures that there's only one instance of a class in the entire application.
- While the basic implementation shown here is straightforward, there are advanced Singleton variations that handle edge cases and thread safety more robustly.

Remember that this exercise introduces you to the Singleton design pattern and its purpose in managing single instances. As you progress, consider exploring more design patterns and their applications in software development.

Exercise 6: RESTful API Client

Develop a C# console application that interacts with a public RESTful API. Fetch and display data using HTTP requests and response handling.

Creating a C# console application that interacts with a public RESTful API is a practical way to learn how to consume external APIs. Here's a step-bystep guide to help you achieve this:

Step 1: Create a New Console Application 1. Open Visual Studio or Visual Studio Code.

2. Create a new console application project.

Step 2: Add Necessary Packages

1. Use NuGet to add the `System.Net.Http` package to your project for making HTTP requests.

Step 3: Choose a RESTful API

1. Choose a public RESTful API that provides data in JSON format.
2. Determine the API endpoint(s) you'll be interacting with.

Step 4: Implement API Interaction

1. In the `Program.cs` file, create a method to interact with the API. 2. Use the `HttpClient` class to make HTTP requests to the API endpoint(s).

Step 5: Deserialize JSON Responses

1. Deserialize the JSON responses received from the API into C# objects using libraries like `System.Text.Json` or `Newtonsoft.Json`.

Step 6: Display Data

1. Process the deserialized objects and display relevant data in the console.

Step 7: Build and Run

1. Build the project.
2. Run the application to see the fetched and displayed data from the public API.

Step 8: Enhancements

1. Handle error responses and exceptions that might occur during API interactions.
2. Experiment with different API endpoints and data manipulation.

Step 9: Testing

1. Test your application with different APIs and endpoints.
2. Observe how your application fetches and displays data in response to API requests.

Additional Notes:

- Interacting with RESTful APIs is a common task in modern software development.
- This guide provides a basic implementation of API interaction. As you progress, consider exploring more advanced topics like authentication, pagination, and data transformation.

Remember that this exercise aims to introduce you to working with RESTful APIs in C#. As you become more familiar with API consumption, you can explore more complex scenarios, error handling, and integration with other parts of your application.

Exercise 7: Polymorphic Animals

Create a base class `Animal` with methods like `Speak()` and `Move()`. Derive classes for specific animals like `Dog`, `Cat`, and `Bird`. Implement their unique behaviors.

Creating a hierarchy of animal classes with polymorphic behaviors is a fun way to understand the concept of polymorphism in object-oriented programming. Here's a step-by-step guide to help you achieve this:

Step 1: Create a New Console Application 1. Open Visual Studio or Visual Studio Code.

2. Create a new console application project.

Step 2: Define Base Animal Class 1. Create a class named `Animal`.

2. Define virtual methods like `Speak()` and `Move()` within the `Animal` class.

Step 3: Create Derived Animal Classes

1. Create classes like `Dog`, `Cat`, and `Bird`, derived from the `Animal` class.
2. Implement the `Speak()` and `Move()` methods with unique behaviors for each animal.

Step 4: Implement Polymorphism

1. In the `Main` method, create an array of `Animal` objects.
2. Instantiate instances of different animal classes and store them in the array.
3. Loop through the array and call the `Speak()` and `Move()` methods for each animal.

Step 5: Build and Run

1. Build the project.
2. Run the application to see how the polymorphic behaviors of different animals are invoked.

Step 6: Enhancements

1. Experiment with more animal classes and behaviors.
2. Explore different ways to organize the animal classes and their behaviors.

Step 7: Testing

1. Test your application by adding new animal classes or modifying the existing ones.
2. Observe how the polymorphic behavior allows you to call methods on objects of different derived classes through a common base class interface.

Additional Notes:

- Polymorphism allows different classes to be treated as instances of a common base class, enabling dynamic behavior based on the actual type of the object.
- This guide provides a basic introduction to polymorphism. As you progress, consider exploring more complex hierarchies and scenarios.

Remember that this exercise introduces you to the concept of polymorphism in a fun and creative way. As you delve deeper into objectoriented programming, you'll encounter various applications of polymorphism and its role in building flexible and extensible software systems.

Exercise 8: File Encryption Utility

Build a C# application that encrypts and decrypts files using a symmetric encryption algorithm like AES. Allow users to provide a password and choose files for encryption.

Creating a file encryption utility using a symmetric encryption algorithm is a practical exercise that can help you understand data security concepts. Here's a step-by-step guide to help you achieve this:

Step 1: Create a New Console Application 1. Open Visual Studio or Visual Studio Code.

2. Create a new console application project.

Step 2: Choose a Symmetric Encryption Algorithm 1. Choose a symmetric encryption algorithm like AES (Advanced Encryption Standard).

2. Familiarize yourself with the algorithm and its usage in C#.

Step 3: Implement Encryption and Decryption

1. In the `Program.cs` file, create methods to encrypt and decrypt files using the chosen algorithm.

2. Use the `AesManaged` class from the `System.Security.Cryptography` namespace to perform encryption and decryption operations.

Step 4: Get User Input

1. Create a user-friendly console interface that prompts the user for a password and the paths to input and output files. 2. Use the `Console.ReadLine()` method to get user input.

Step 5: Encrypt and Decrypt Files

1. Implement the logic to read the input file, encrypt its contents using the chosen algorithm, and write the encrypted data to the output file.
2. Implement the reverse process to decrypt the encrypted file back to its original form.

Step 6: Build and Run

1. Build the project.
2. Run the application to encrypt and decrypt files using the provided password and file paths.

Step 7: Enhancements

1. Implement error handling for file operations and encryption/decryption processes.
2. Experiment with different encryption algorithms and modes.

Step 8: Testing

1. Test your application with different files and passwords.
2. Verify that the encrypted file is unreadable without proper decryption.

Additional Notes:

- Implementing file encryption helps you understand the importance of securing sensitive data.
- This guide provides a basic introduction to file encryption. Consider exploring more advanced topics like key management and secure storage.

Remember that this exercise introduces you to the concept of file encryption using symmetric encryption algorithms. As you delve further into security and cryptography, you'll encounter more complex algorithms, best practices, and encryption techniques used in real-world applications.

Exercise 9: Dependency Injection with ASP.NET MVC

Extend a previous ASP.NET MVC web application to utilize dependency injection for services. Use an IoC container like Autofac or Microsoft.Extensions.DependencyInjection.

Implementing dependency injection in an ASP.NET MVC web application is a valuable exercise to learn about the benefits of loose coupling and managing dependencies. Here's a step-by-step guide to help you achieve this:

Step 1: Create a New ASP.NET MVC Web Application

1. Open Visual Studio.
2. Create a new ASP.NET MVC web application project.

Step 2: Choose an IoC Container

1. Choose an IoC (Inversion of Control) container like Autofac or Microsoft.Extensions.DependencyInjection.
2. Install the chosen IoC container package using NuGet.

Step 3: Define Services and Interfaces

1. Create interfaces for the services you want to inject.
2. Implement concrete classes that implement these interfaces.

Step 4: Configure Dependency Injection

1. Configure the IoC container to register your services and their implementations.
2. Set up the IoC container to work with ASP.NET MVC's dependency resolver.

Step 5: Inject Services into Controllers

1. Modify your controllers to accept interface parameters for the services they depend on.
2. Use constructor injection to pass the services to the controllers.

Step 6: Build and Run

1. Build the project.
2. Run the application to see how dependency injection is used to provide services to controllers.

Step 7: Enhancements

1. Experiment with different IoC containers and compare their features. 2. Implement more complex service configurations, such as scoped and transient lifetimes.

Step 8: Testing

1. Test your application to ensure that services are properly injected and used by the controllers.
2. Verify that dependency injection leads to more maintainable and modular code.

Additional Notes:

- Dependency injection improves code maintainability, testability, and flexibility by decoupling components.
- This guide provides a basic introduction to dependency injection in ASP.NET MVC. As you progress, consider exploring more advanced topics like aspect-oriented programming and cross-cutting concerns.

Remember that this exercise introduces you to the concept of dependency injection in the context of web applications. As you continue to develop software, you'll find that proper dependency management is crucial for building scalable and maintainable applications.

Exercise 10: Observer Pattern in UI

Create a C# WPF application that demonstrates the Observer pattern. Implement a simple notification system where one component notifies others about state changes.

Implementing the Observer pattern in a WPF application is a great way to understand how components can communicate and respond to changes. Here's a step-by-step guide to help you achieve this:

Step 1: Create a New WPF Application 1. Open Visual Studio.

2. Create a new WPF application project.

Step 2: Define Subject and Observer Interfaces

1. Define an `ISubject` interface with methods to attach, detach, and notify observers.
2. Define an `IObserver` interface with a method to update when the subject's state changes.

Step 3: Implement Subject and Observer Classes

1. Create a class that implements the `ISubject` interface. This will manage a list of observers and notify them of state changes.
2. Create classes that implement the `IObserver` interface. These classes will respond to state changes by updating their content.

Step 4: Create WPF Components

1. Design your WPF window with components that represent the subject and observers.
2. Add buttons or triggers to simulate state changes that will trigger notifications.

Step 5: Wire Up Components

1. In the code-behind, create instances of the subject and observer classes.
2. Attach the observer instances to the subject.
3. Handle button clicks or triggers to change the subject's state and notify observers.

Step 6: Build and Run

1. Build the project.
2. Run the application to see how the observer pattern works in the context of a WPF application.

Step 7: Enhancements

1. Implement different types of observers that respond to state changes differently.
2. Experiment with more complex scenarios where multiple observers respond to changes in different ways.

Step 8: Testing

1. Test your application by triggering state changes and observing how the observers respond.
2. Verify that the observer pattern enables components to communicate without tight coupling.

Additional Notes:

- The Observer pattern is a fundamental design pattern that promotes loose coupling between components.
- This guide provides a basic introduction to implementing the Observer pattern in a WPF application. As you continue working with UI and eventdriven programming, you'll encounter more advanced scenarios and patterns.

Remember that this exercise introduces you to the Observer pattern and its application in a user interface context. As you explore more patterns and architectural principles, you'll find that the Observer pattern is just one of the many tools available for building modular and responsive software systems.

Exercise 11: Advanced ASP.NET Core Web API

Extend the Web API from a previous exercise to support token-based authentication and authorization using JWT (JSON Web Tokens).

Adding token-based authentication and authorization to an ASP.NET Core Web API is a valuable exercise to understand how to secure your APIs. Here's a step-by-step guide to helpyou achieve this:

Step 1: Extend the Existing Web API

1. Start with the existing ASP.NET Core Web API project you created in a previous exercise.

Step 2: Install Required Packages

1. Install the necessary NuGet packages for JWT authentication and authorization.

Step 3: Configure Authentication and Authorization 1. Configure JWT authentication in the `Startup.cs` file using the `AddAuthentication` and `AddJwtBearer` methods.

2. Set up authorization policies using the `AddAuthorization` method. Define roles and policies as needed.

Step 4: Generate JWT Tokens

1. Implement a token generation service that creates JWT tokens when a user successfully logs in.
2. Customize the token's claims, expiration time, and other attributes as required.

Step 5: Secure Controllers and Actions

1. Apply `[Authorize]` attributes to controllers or actions that require authentication and authorization.
2. Use `[AllowAnonymous]` attribute on actions that should be accessible without authentication.

Step 6: Test Token-Based Authentication

1. Use tools like Postman to send requests to your API endpoints.
2. Include the generated JWT token in the request headers for protected routes.

Step 7: Enhancements

1. Customize error responses for unauthorized access or expired tokens.
2. Implement role-based authorization and fine-grained access control.

Step 8: Testing

1. Test your API endpoints with valid and invalid tokens to ensure proper authentication and authorization.
2. Verify that protected routes are accessible only with valid tokens.

Additional Notes:

- Token-based authentication using JWT is a powerful method for securing APIs and controlling access.
- This guide provides a basic introduction to implementing token-based authentication and authorization in an ASP.NET Core Web API. As you continue developing secure applications, you'll encounter more advanced security techniques and considerations.

Remember that this exercise introduces you to token-based authentication and authorization using JWT. As you progress, consider exploring other security features, such as refresh tokens, token revocation, and user roles and claims. Security is a critical aspect of modern software development, and understanding authentication and authorization is essential for building secure and trustworthy applications.

Exercise 12: Complex Design Patterns

Choose a complex design pattern (such as Composite, Interpreter, or Mediator) and implement it in a real-world scenario using C#.

Here's a step-by-step guide to creating a C# program that simulates memory management by implementing a custom memory allocator with methods to allocate and deallocate memory blocks, while handling fragmentation:

Step 1: Create a New C# Console Application

Open your preferred development environment (such as Visual Studio) and create a new C# console application project. Name the project, solution, and main class, such as `MemoryAllocatorSimulation`.

Step 2: Define the MemoryBlock Class Define a class to represent a memory block:

```csharp
class MemoryBlock

{ public int Size { get; set; } public bool IsAllocated { get; set; } public MemoryBlock Next { get; set; }

}
```

Step 3: Create the MemoryAllocator Class

Create a class for the memory allocator with methods to allocate and deallocate memory blocks:

```csharp

class MemoryAllocator

{ private MemoryBlock head;

public MemoryAllocator(int totalSize)

{ head = new MemoryBlock { Size = totalSize, IsAllocated = false,

Next = null }; }

public void Allocate(int size)

{

MemoryBlock current = head; while (current != null)

{ if (!current.IsAllocated && current.Size >= size)
```

```
{ current.IsAllocated = true; if (current.Size > size)
{
MemoryBlock newBlock = new MemoryBlock { Size =
current.Size - size, IsAllocated = false, Next = current.Next };
current.Size = size; current.Next = newBlock;
}
return; }
current = current.Next;
}
Console.WriteLine("Memory allocation failed. No suitable block found."); }
public void Deallocate()
{
MemoryBlock current = head; while (current != null)
{
if (current.IsAllocated)
{ current.IsAllocated = false; // Merge adjacent free blocks
if (current.Next != null && !current.Next.IsAllocated)
{ current.Size += current.Next.Size; current.Next = current.Next.Next;
}
}
current = current.Next;
}
}
public void DisplayMemory()
```

```
{
MemoryBlock current = head;
while (current != null)
{
Console.Write($"[{(current.IsAllocated ? "X" : " ")}:{current.Size}]
");
current = current.Next;
}
Console.WriteLine();
}
}
```

Step 4: Create the Main Program

Write the `Main` method to test the memory allocator:

```csharp
class Program
{
static void Main(string[] args)
{
MemoryAllocator allocator = new MemoryAllocator(100);
allocator.DisplayMemory(); allocator.Allocate(30); allocator.DisplayMemory(); allocator.Allocate(20); allocator.DisplayMemory(); allocator.Deallocate(); allocator.DisplayMemory(); allocator.Allocate(15);
allocator.DisplayMemory();
}
}
```

Step 5: Compile and Run

Build and run your C# console application in your development environment.

Step 6: Observe Output

You should see the program simulating memory allocation and deallocation, as well as displaying the memory blocks and their allocation status.

Congratulations! You've successfully created a C# program that simulates memory management by implementing a custom memory allocator with methods to allocate and deallocate memory blocks, while handling fragmentation.

Exercise 13: Parallel Programming

Develop a program that performs parallel processing using the Task Parallel Library (TPL) to process a large dataset efficiently.

Here's a step-by-step guide to creating a C# program that performs parallel processing using the Task Parallel Library (TPL) to efficiently process a large dataset:

Step 1: Create a New C# Console Application

Open your preferred development environment (such as Visual Studio) and create a new C# console application project. Name the project, solution, and main class, such as `ParallelProcessing`.

Step 2: Define the Data Processing Logic

Define the data processing logic that you want to perform in parallel. For this example, let's say you want to calculate the square of each number in a large dataset.

```csharp
using System;

using System.Threading.Tasks;

class Program

{

static void Main(string[] args)

{

// Create a large dataset int[] data = new int[1000000]; for (int i = 0; i < data.Length; i++)
```

```
{ data[i] = i + 1;

}

// Process data in parallel

Parallel.For(0, data.Length, i =>

{ data[i] = data[i] * data[i]; // Square each number

});

Console.WriteLine("Data processing completed."); }

}
```

Step 3: Compile and Run

Build and run your C# console application in your development environment.

Step 4: Observe Output

You should see the program processing the large dataset by squaring each number in parallel using the TPL.

Congratulations! You've successfully created a C# program that performs parallel processing using the Task Parallel Library (TPL) to efficiently process a large dataset.

Exercise 14: Custom ORM

Build a simple Object-Relational Mapping (ORM) framework that allows developers to map C# objects to database tables and perform basic CRUD operations.

Building a complete Object-Relational Mapping (ORM) framework is quite extensive, but I can provide you with a simplified example of how you might implement a basic ORM for mapping C# objects to database tables and performing CRUD operations.

Please note that a real-world ORM framework involves many more features and considerations, such as connection pooling, transaction management, query optimization, and more.

Step 1: Create a New C# Console Application

Open your preferred development environment (such as Visual Studio) and create a new C# console application project. Name the project, solution, and main class, such as `CustomORM`.

Step 2: Define the Object Mapping Attributes

Define custom attributes to associate C# classes with database tables and columns:

```csharp
using System;

[AttributeUsage(AttributeTargets.Class)] class TableAttribute : Attribute

{ public string TableName { get; }

public TableAttribute(string tableName)

{

TableName = tableName;

}

}

[AttributeUsage(AttributeTargets.Property)] class ColumnAttribute : Attribute

{ public string ColumnName { get; }

public ColumnAttribute(string columnName)

{

ColumnName = columnName;

}

}
```

Step 3: Create a Simple ORM Framework

Implement a simple ORM framework with methods for CRUD operations:

```csharp
using System; using System.Reflection; using System.Data.SqlClient;

class CustomORM

{ private readonly SqlConnection connection; public CustomORM(string connectionString)

{ connection = new SqlConnection(connectionString); connection.Open();
```

```
}
public void Insert(object obj)
{
Type type = obj.GetType(); string tableName = GetTableName(type);
PropertyInfo[] properties = type.GetProperties(); string columns = string.Join(", ", properties.Select(p =>
GetColumnName(p))); string values = string.Join(", ", properties.Select(p =>
$"@{p.Name}"));
using (SqlCommand command = new SqlCommand($"INSERT
INTO {tableName} ({columns}) VALUES ({values})", connection))
{ foreach (PropertyInfo property in properties)
{ command.Parameters.AddWithValue($"@{property.Name}", property.GetValue(obj));
}
command.ExecuteNonQuery();
}
}
// Implement Update, Delete, and Select methods similarly
private string GetTableName(Type type)
{
TableAttribute tableAttribute = type.GetCustomAttribute<TableAttribute>(); if (tableAttribute != null)
{ return tableAttribute.TableName;
}
throw new Exception("TableAttribute not found."); }
private string GetColumnName(PropertyInfo property)
{
```

ColumnAttribute columnAttribute = property.GetCustomAttribute<ColumnAttribute>(); if (columnAttribute != null)

{ return columnAttribute.ColumnName;

}

return property.Name;

}

}

```

Step 4: Use the Custom ORM

Use the custom ORM framework to map C# objects to database tables and perform CRUD operations:

```csharp class Program

{

static void Main(string[] args)

{ string connectionString = "your_connection_string_here";

CustomORM orm = new CustomORM(connectionString);

// Example class and attributes [Table("Employees")] class Employee

{

[Column("Id")]

public int EmployeeId { get; set; }

[Column("Name")]

public string EmployeeName { get; set; }

}

Employee newEmployee = new Employee

{

```
EmployeeId = 1,

EmployeeName = "John Doe"

}; orm.Insert(newEmployee);

// Perform other CRUD operations as needed

Console.WriteLine("CRUD operations completed."); }

}
```

Step 5: Compile and Run

Build and run your C# console application in your development environment. Make sure to replace `"your_connection_string_here"` with your actual database connection string.

Step 6: Observe Output

You should see the program using the custom ORM framework to perform CRUD operations on the specified database table.

Please note that this example is quite simplified and lacks error handling, query generation, and other essential features of a full-fledged ORM framework. Building a production-ready ORM is a complex task and involves considerations beyond this basic example.

Exercise 15: Machine Learning Integration

Integrate a machine learning model (e.g., TensorFlow or ML.NET) into a C# application to perform a specific task, such as image recognition or sentiment analysis.

Integrating a machine learning model into a C# application involves multiple steps. Here's a step-by-step guide to help you integrate a machine learning model (using TensorFlow and ML.NET as examples) into a C# application for image recognition:

Step 1: Create a New C# Console Application

Open your preferred development environment (such as Visual Studio) and create a new C# console application project. Name the project, solution, and main class, such as `MLIntegration`.

Step 2: Set Up Your Environment

You'll need to install necessary packages to work with TensorFlow and

ML.NET. In Visual Studio, right-click on your project in the Solution Explorer and select "Manage NuGet Packages." Search for and install the required packages, such as `TensorFlow.NET` and `Microsoft.ML`.

Step 3: Load and Prepare the Model For TensorFlow:

1. Download a pre-trained TensorFlow model (e.g., for image recognition).
2. Load the model in your C# application using TensorFlow.NET.

For ML.NET:

1. Create and train an ML.NET model (e.g., for sentiment analysis) using available datasets.
2. Save the trained model to a file.

Step 4: Use the Model in Your Application For TensorFlow:

1. Use the loaded model to make predictions on input data.
2. Process the prediction results to perform the desired task.

For ML.NET:

1. Load the trained ML.NET model from the file.
2. Create a prediction engine using the loaded model.
3. Use the prediction engine to make predictions on input data.

Step 5: Integrate Model with Input Data For TensorFlow:

1. Preprocess input data (e.g., images) to match the model's input format.
2. Pass the preprocessed data to the model for prediction.

For ML.NET:

1. Create an input data object with the required fields.
2. Use the prediction engine to make predictions on the input data object.

Step 6: Display Results For TensorFlow:

1. Process the prediction results to identify the predicted classes or labels.
2. Display the prediction results to the user.

For ML.NET:

1. Interpret the prediction results (e.g., sentiment score).
2. Display the interpretation or decision based on the prediction.

Step 7: Compile and Run

Build and run your C# console application in your development environment.

Step 8: Observe Output

You should see the program using the integrated machine learning model to perform the specific task (image recognition or sentiment analysis) based on the input data.

Note and Additional Steps:

- Please note that integrating machine learning models involves more specific code depending on the chosen model and task.
- TensorFlow and ML.NET have extensive documentation and tutorials that guide you through the integration process for different use cases. - Make sure to follow the documentation of the chosen machine learning library to ensure proper implementation and accuracy.

Remember that this is a simplified guide, and actual integration can vary based on your chosen model, task, and libraries.

Exercise 16: Advanced Dependency Injection

Extend a previous dependency injection project by implementing more advanced features like transient and scoped service lifetimes. Explore aspects like managing service instances.

Here's a step-by-step guide to extending a previous dependency injection project by implementing more advanced features like transient and scoped service lifetimes, as well as managing service instances:

Step 1: Build on Existing Dependency Injection Setup

Assuming you already have a basic dependency injection setup, let's extend it to handle advanced scenarios.

Step 2: Implement Transient Lifetime

Transient lifetime means a new instance of a service is created every time it's requested. To implement this:

1. Modify your service registration code to use `.AddTransient<IService, ServiceImplementation>()` for transient services.
2. Now, every time a service is requested, a new instance will be created.

Step 3: Implement Scoped Lifetime

Scoped lifetime means a single instance of a service is created for the duration of a "scope," which typically represents a unit of work or an HTTP request. To implement this:

1. Modify your service registration code to use `.AddScoped<IService, ServiceImplementation>()` for scoped services.
2. Ensure you're setting up a scope correctly (e.g., using ASP.NET Core's built-in mechanism for web requests).

Step 4: Managing Service Instances

To manage service instances, you might want to understand how the dependency injection container works under the hood:

1. Dependency injection containers store registered services and their lifetimes.
2. When a service is requested, the container checks its lifetime to decide whether to create a new instance or return an existing one.

Step 5: Compile and Run

Build and run your application with the advanced dependency injection features.

Step 6: Observe Behavior

Create scenarios to test the behavior of transient and scoped services: - For transient services, request the service multiple times and observe different instances being created.

- For scoped services, simulate a unit of work (e.g., an HTTP request) and observe that the same instance is reused within that scope.

Additional Notes:

- Advanced dependency injection features can be more relevant in larger applications where you need to control the lifetime of services for better performance and resource management.
- While this example provides a basic understanding, real-world scenarios can involve more complex setups and considerations.

Remember that this guide provides a simplified overview of advanced dependency injection features. Implementations can vary based on the framework you're using and the specific requirements of your application.

Exercise 17: Cryptocurrency Blockchain

Develop a simple blockchain for a cryptocurrency using C#. Implement features like mining, transactions, and chain validation.

Here's a step-by-step guide to developing a simple blockchain for a cryptocurrency using C#, implementing features like mining, transactions, and chain validation:

Step 1: Create a New C# Console Application

Open your preferred development environment (such as Visual Studio) and create a new C# console application project. Name the project, solution, and main class, such as `CryptocurrencyBlockchain`.

Step 2: Define the Block and Blockchain Classes Define classes for a block and the blockchain itself:

```csharp
using System;

using System.Collections.Generic;

class Block

{ public int Index { get; set; } public DateTime Timestamp { get; set; } public string PreviousHash { get; set; } public string Hash { get; set; } public int Nonce { get; set; }

public List<Transaction> Transactions { get; set; }

}

class Transaction

{ public string FromAddress { get; set; } public string ToAddress { get; set; } public int Amount { get; set; }

}
```

Step 3: Implement Mining

Implement a method to mine a new block:

```csharp

class CryptocurrencyBlockchain

{ private List<Block> blockchain = new List<Block>(); private int difficulty = 2;

public Block CreateGenesisBlock()

{ return new Block

{

Index = 0,

Timestamp = DateTime.Now,
```

```
PreviousHash = "0",

Hash = CalculateHash(0, DateTime.Now, "0"),

Nonce = 0,

Transactions = new List<Transaction>()

}; }

public Block MineBlock(Block previousBlock, List<Transaction>
transactions)

{ int index = previousBlock.Index + 1; DateTime timestamp = DateTime.Now; string previousHash =
previousBlock.Hash;

int nonce = 0;

string hash = CalculateHash(index, timestamp, previousHash,

transactions, nonce);

while (!hash.StartsWith(new string('0', difficulty)))

{ nonce++;

hash = CalculateHash(index, timestamp, previousHash,

transactions, nonce);

}

return new Block

{

Index = index,

Timestamp = timestamp,

PreviousHash = previousHash,

Hash = hash,

Nonce = nonce,
```

```
Transactions = transactions
};
}
}
```

Step 4: Implement Chain Validation

Implement a method to validate the integrity of the blockchain:

```csharp
class CryptocurrencyBlockchain
{
// Previous code...
public bool IsChainValid()
{ for (int i = 1; i < blockchain.Count; i++)
{
Block currentBlock = blockchain[i]; Block previousBlock = blockchain[i - 1];
if (currentBlock.Hash != CalculateHash(currentBlock.Index,
currentBlock.Timestamp,
currentBlock.PreviousHash, currentBlock.Transactions,
currentBlock.Nonce) || currentBlock.PreviousHash != previousBlock.Hash)
{
return false;
}
} return true;
}
```

}

```

Step 5: Compile and Run

Build and run your C# console application in your development environment.

Step 6: Observe Blockchain Behavior

Create transactions and mine blocks to see how the blockchain grows and how mining works.

Please note that this is a simplified example of a cryptocurrency blockchain. Real-world blockchains involve additional features like consensus algorithms, peer-to-peer networking, and more complex cryptographic functions.

**Exercise 18:** Real-Time Data Visualization

Create a real-time data visualization application using a C# framework like LiveCharts. Display dynamic data streams in various chart types.

Here's a step-by-step guide to creating a real-time data visualization application using a C# framework like LiveCharts to display dynamic data streams in various chart types:

Step 1: Set Up Your Environment

1. Open your preferred development environment (such as Visual Studio). 2. Create a new C# WPF application project. Name the project, solution, and main class, such as `RealTimeDataVisualization`.

Step 2: Install LiveCharts

1. Right-click on your project in the Solution Explorer and select "Manage NuGet Packages."
2. Search for and install the `LiveCharts.Wpf` package.

Step 3: Design the User Interface

1. Open the `MainWindow.xaml` file and design your user interface. Place a `CartesianChart` control where you want to display the real-time data visualization.

Step 4: Initialize Data Series

1. In the code-behind (`MainWindow.xaml.cs`), create an instance of `SeriesCollection` to hold your data series.

Step 5: Generate and Display Real-Time Data
```

1. Use a timer (such as `DispatcherTimer`) to generate random data points at regular intervals.
2. Add the generated data points to your data series.
3. Update the chart to display the latest data.

Step 6: Choose Chart Types

1. Customize the appearance of your chart by selecting various chart types, colors, and styles.
2. Explore different types like line charts, bar charts, pie charts, etc.

Step 7: Compile and Run

Build and run your WPF application in your development environment.

Step 8: Observe Real-Time Data Visualization

As the timer generates random data points, you should see the real-time data visualization updating on the chart.

Additional Notes:

- LiveCharts offers a variety of chart types and customization options. Refer to the LiveCharts documentation for more information on how to use its features.
- For more complex real-time data, you might need to fetch data from an external source (e.g., API, database) and update the chart accordingly.

Remember that this guide provides a basic overview of creating a real-time data visualization application using LiveCharts. Depending on your requirements and the specific chart library you choose, implementations can vary.

Exercise 19: Speech Recognition Application

Build a speech recognition application using C# that converts spoken words into text. Utilize libraries like Microsoft's Speech SDK.

Here's a step-by-step guide to building a speech recognition application using C# that converts spoken words into text, utilizing libraries like Microsoft's Speech SDK:

Step 1: Set Up Your Environment

1. Open your preferred development environment (such as Visual Studio).
2. Create a new C# Windows Forms application project. Name the project, solution, and main form class, such as `SpeechRecognitionApp`.

Step 2: Install Microsoft Speech SDK

1. Right-click on your project in the Solution Explorer and select "Manage NuGet Packages."

2. Search for and install the

`Microsoft.CognitiveServices.SpeechRecognizer` package.

Step 3: Design the User Interface

1. Open the main form designer (`Form1.Designer.cs`) and design your user interface. Add a `TextBox` to display the recognized speech.

Step 4: Initialize the Speech Recognizer

1. In the code-behind (`Form1.cs`), import the necessary namespaces.
2. Create a `SpeechRecognizer` instance using your subscription key and service region.

Step 5: Handle Recognition Events

1. Subscribe to the `Recognized` event of the `SpeechRecognizer` to handle recognized speech.
2. In the event handler, update the `TextBox` with the recognized text.

Step 6: Implement Start and Stop Buttons

1. Add "Start" and "Stop" buttons to your form.
2. In the "Start" button click event, start the speech recognition. 3. In the "Stop" button click event, stop the speech recognition.

Step 7: Compile and Run

Build and run your Windows Forms application in your development environment.

Step 8: Test Speech Recognition

Click the "Start" button, speak into your microphone, and you should see the recognized text displayed in the `TextBox`.

Additional Notes:

- Microsoft's Speech SDK offers more advanced features, such as language customization and continuous recognition. Refer to the SDK documentation for more information.
- Make sure to handle error cases, such as microphone not available or recognition failing.

Remember that this guide provides a basic overview of building a speech recognition application using Microsoft's Speech SDK. Depending on your requirements and the specific library you choose, implementations can vary.

Exercise 20: Natural Language Processing

Implement a basic natural language processing (NLP) application in C#. Use libraries like Stanford NLP or SpaCy to perform tasks like sentiment analysis or entity recognition.

Here's a step-by-step guide to implementing a basic natural language processing (NLP) application in C# using libraries like Stanford NLP or SpaCy to perform tasks like sentiment analysis or entity recognition:

Step 1: Set Up Your Environment

1. Open your preferred development environment (such as Visual Studio).
2. Create a new C# console application project. Name the project, solution, and main class, such as `NLPApplication`.

Step 2: Install NLP Libraries

1. Depending on the library you choose (e.g., Stanford NLP or SpaCy), install the appropriate NuGet packages for NLP.
2. Follow the documentation of the library to set up the required resources and models.

Step 3: Implement Sentiment Analysis

1. In the code-behind (`Program.cs`), import the necessary namespaces.
2. Use the NLP library's API to perform sentiment analysis on a given text.
3. Display the sentiment score or label to the user.

Step 4: Implement Entity Recognition

1. Extend your application to perform entity recognition using the NLP library.
2. Extract named entities (such as people, organizations, locations) from a text.
3. Display the extracted entities to the user.

Step 5: Compile and Run

Build and run your C# console application in your development environment.

Step 6: Test NLP Tasks

Input various text samples into your application and observe the sentiment analysis scores or the recognized entities.

Additional Notes:

- Different NLP libraries might have different APIs and usage patterns.

Consult the documentation of the chosen library for details. - NLP tasks can be resource-intensive. Ensure you're following best practices to optimize performance.

Remember that this guide provides a basic overview of building an NLP application using libraries like Stanford NLP or SpaCy. Depending on your requirements and the specific library you choose, implementations can vary.

Exercise 21: Distributed Systems

Build a distributed computing system using C# that communicates across multiple nodes. Implement message passing, load balancing, and fault tolerance.

Building a distributed computing system is a complex task, but here's a high-level step-by-step guide to get you started with the concepts using C#:

Step 1: Set Up Your Environment

1. Open your preferred development environment (such as Visual Studio).
2. Create a new solution and multiple C# projects for each node in your distributed system. Name the projects accordingly, like `Node1`, `Node2`, etc.

Step 2: Implement Message Passing

1. Choose a communication mechanism like sockets or HTTP APIs for nodes to exchange messages.
2. In each node's project, implement code to send and receive messages.
3. Define a protocol for message format and encoding.

Step 3: Implement Load Balancing

1. Designate a central node as a load balancer.
2. Implement code in the load balancer to distribute incoming tasks/messages among available nodes.
3. Nodes should periodically report their load status to the load balancer.

Step 4: Implement Fault Tolerance

1. Define scenarios that might lead to node failures (e.g., crashes, network issues).
2. Implement mechanisms like heartbeats or timeouts to detect failed nodes.
3. Design the system to automatically redistribute tasks to healthy nodes.

Step 5: Compile and Run

Build and run each node's project in your development environment.

Step 6: Test Distributed System

Simulate different scenarios to test message passing, load balancing, and fault tolerance. For example, start and stop nodes to observe how tasks are distributed and handled.

Additional Notes:

- Building a full-fledged distributed system involves more complex considerations like data consistency, synchronization, security, and more. - Distributed systems are typically built using frameworks and technologies designed for this purpose, such as Apache Kafka, RabbitMQ, or Kubernetes.
- Consider using libraries and frameworks that provide abstractions for distributed systems to handle some of the complexities.

Remember that this guide provides a high-level overview of building a basic distributed computing system using C#. The actual implementation can vary significantly based on your requirements and the technologies you choose.

Exercise 22: Real-Time Game Development

Develop a real-time game using a game engine like Unity or MonoGame. Implement complex gameplay mechanics, physics, and multiplayer networking.

Here's a high-level step-by-step guide to developing a real-time game using a game engine like Unity or MonoGame, implementing complex gameplay mechanics, physics, and multiplayer networking:

Step 1: Choose a Game Engine

1. Decide whether you'll use Unity or MonoGame as your game engine.
2. Set up the chosen engine and create a new project for your game.

Step 2: Design Gameplay Mechanics

1. Define the core gameplay mechanics and features of your game.
2. Design the rules, controls, interactions, and objectives.

Step 3: Implement Physics and Mechanics

1. Utilize the physics engine of the game engine to simulate realistic physics interactions.
2. Implement player movements, collisions, and interactions based on your game's mechanics.

Step 4: Develop Graphics and Assets

1. Create or import 2D/3D assets, characters, objects, and environments for your game.
2. Design levels and scenes using the engine's tools.

Step 5: Implement Multiplayer Networking

1. If your game supports multiplayer, implement network code for player interactions.
2. Choose a networking library or framework compatible with your game engine.

Step 6: Compile and Test

1. Build and run your game within the game engine's environment.

2. Test gameplay, mechanics, physics, and multiplayer interactions.

Step 7: Iterate and Optimize

1. Playtest your game to identify bugs, balance issues, and areas for improvement.
2. Make adjustments, optimizations, and refinements based on feedback.

Step 8: Polish and Release

1. Fine-tune visuals, audio, and overall experience.
2. Once satisfied, prepare your game for release on the chosen platform(s).

Step 9: Distribute and Showcase

1. Distribute your game to platforms such as PC, console, or mobile.
2. Showcase your game on platforms like game distribution platforms, social media, or your own website.

Additional Notes:

- Developing a real-time game is a comprehensive endeavor that involves design, programming, graphics, sound, and more.
- Unity and MonoGame offer extensive documentation and community resources to guide you through game development.
- Complex multiplayer games may require backend server architecture and services for synchronization, matchmaking, etc.

Remember that this guide provides a high-level overview of developing a real-time game using a game engine. The actual implementation can be intricate and might require deep understanding and experience in game development.

Exercise 23: Neural Network Implementation

Create a neural network library in C# from scratch. Implement forward and backward propagation, gradient descent, and activation functions.

Developing a neural network library from scratch is a complex task. Here's a high-level step-by-step guide to get you started with the concepts in C#:

Step 1: Set Up Your Environment

1. Open your preferred development environment (such as Visual Studio). 2. Create a new C# class library project. Name the project, solution, and main class, such as `NeuralNetworkLibrary`.

Step 2: Design Neural Network Components

1. Define the structure of the neural network, including layers, neurons, and connections.
2. Decide on the number of input and output neurons, hidden layers, and activation functions.

Step 3: Implement Activation Functions

1. Implement common activation functions like sigmoid, ReLU, etc., as separate classes.
2. Add methods to calculate activations and their derivatives.

Step 4: Implement Forward Propagation

1. Implement a method to perform forward propagation through the neural network.
2. Calculate outputs of each neuron using weighted inputs and activation functions.

Step 5: Implement Backward Propagation

1. Implement a method to perform backward propagation to calculate gradients.
2. Calculate gradients of weights and biases using the chain rule.

Step 6: Implement Gradient Descent

1. Implement a method to update weights and biases using gradient descent.
2. Adjust weights and biases based on calculated gradients and learning rate.

Step 7: Compile and Test

1. Build the class library project in your development environment.
2. Create a separate console application to test your neural network library.

Step 8: Test Neural Network

1. Create a small dataset for training and testing.
2. Use your neural network library to train and predict on the dataset.
3. Observe how the network's accuracy improves through iterations.

Additional Notes:

- Developing a neural network library involves advanced concepts in mathematics and machine learning.
- This guide provides a basic outline; actual implementation requires deep knowledge of neural networks and optimization algorithms.

Remember that this guide provides a high-level overview of building a neural network library in C#. The actual implementation involves a deep understanding of neural networks, backpropagation, gradient descent, and related concepts.

Exercise 24: High-Performance Computing

Write a C# program that utilizes GPU acceleration using libraries like CUDA or OpenCL for massive parallel processing tasks.

Utilizing GPU acceleration for high-performance computing tasks is an advanced topic. Here's a high-level step-by-step guide to get you started with GPU acceleration using libraries like CUDA or OpenCL in C#:

Step 1: Choose a GPU Acceleration Library

1. Decide whether you'll use CUDA or OpenCL for GPU acceleration. 2. Install the necessary development tools and libraries for the chosen library.

Step 2: Set Up Your Environment

1. Open your preferred development environment (such as Visual Studio).
2. Create a new C# console application project. Name the project, solution, and main class, such as `GPUAccelerationApp`.

Step 3: Import GPU Libraries

1. Import the necessary namespaces and references for the chosen GPU library.
2. Set up the environment to work with GPU-accelerated code.

Step 4: Write Parallel Code

1. Identify a computationally intensive task that can be parallelized.
2. Implement the parallel code using the GPU library's APIs and syntax.
3. Divide the task into smaller parallel threads or blocks.

Step 5: Compile and Run

1. Build and run your C# console application in your development environment.
2. Observe the performance improvements achieved through GPU acceleration.

Step 6: Test and Optimize

1. Test your GPU-accelerated code with different input sizes.
2. Profile your code to identify bottlenecks and optimize for better performance.

Additional Notes:

- GPU acceleration requires a good understanding of parallel programming and the specific GPU library you're using.
- GPU programming is specialized and often involves working with lowlevel APIs and memory management.

Remember that this guide provides a high-level overview of utilizing GPU acceleration using libraries like CUDA or OpenCL in C#. The actual implementation can be complex and requires a deep understanding of GPU architecture and parallel programming techniques.

Exercise 25: Advanced IoT Application

Build an Internet of Things (IoT) application using C#. Connect and control multiple IoT devices, process sensor data, and implement real-time monitoring and alerts.

Developing an advanced Internet of Things (IoT) application is a complex task. Here's a high-level step-by-step guide to get you started with the concepts using C#:

Step 1: Define the IoT Application

1. Clearly define the purpose and objectives of your IoT application.
2. Determine the types of IoT devices you'll be connecting and controlling.

Step 2: Choose IoT Protocols and Platforms

1. Decide on communication protocols such as MQTT, CoAP, HTTP, etc. 2. Choose an IoT platform for device management, data processing, and visualization.

Step 3: Set Up Your Environment

1. Open your preferred development environment (such as Visual Studio).
2. Create a new solution and projects for different components of your IoT application.

Step 4: Connect and Control IoT Devices

1. Implement code to establish communication with IoT devices using the chosen protocol.
2. Implement control mechanisms to send commands and receive data from devices.

Step 5: Process Sensor Data

1. Implement code to process and analyze sensor data received from IoT devices.
2. Apply relevant algorithms and logic to derive insights from the data.

Step 6: Implement Real-Time Monitoring

1. Set up real-time data monitoring using visualization tools or dashboards.
2. Display the sensor data and status of connected devices in real-time.

Step 7: Implement Alerts and Notifications

1. Implement code to trigger alerts and notifications based on predefined conditions.
2. Utilize email, SMS, or push notifications to inform users of critical events.

Step 8: Compile and Test

1. Build and run the different components of your IoT application in your development environment.
2. Simulate device data or connect actual IoT devices for testing.

Step 9: Test IoT Functionality

1. Test device connectivity, data processing, real-time monitoring, and alerts.
2. Verify that the application responds as expected to different scenarios.

Step 10: Optimize and Deploy

1. Optimize the performance of your IoT application for efficiency and reliability.
2. Deploy your IoT application to a target environment (cloud, onpremises, etc.).

Additional Notes:

- Developing a comprehensive IoT application involves considerations for security, scalability, and interoperability.
- IoT platforms like Azure IoT, AWS IoT, or Google Cloud IoT offer tools to simplify IoT application development.

Remember that this guide provides a high-level overview of building an advanced IoT application using C#. The actual implementation can be intricate and might require expertise in IoT protocols, data processing, and cloud services.

Don't forget to scan the QR Code to get all bonus content!

Made in the USA
Monee, IL
09 March 2024